# THE COASTERS

by

Bill Millar



A STAR BOOK
*published by*
W. H. ALLEN

A Star Book
Published in 1975
by W. H. Allen & Co. Ltd.
44, Hill Street, London, W1X 8LB



Printed in Great Britain by
Richard Clay (The Chaucer Press), Ltd., Bungay, Suffolk

ISBN 0 352 30020 5

# THE COASTERS

is an original
Star Books paperback edition

Bill Millar, a London civil servant, took a keen interest in R & B and Rock 'n' Roll on leaving school. Following his first article for *Blues Unlimited* in 1965, he has written for many leading specialist magazines including *Shout* and *Bim Bam Boom*. His previous book, THE DRIFTERS: THE RISE AND FALL OF THE BLACK VOCAL GROUP, was widely acclaimed in 1971 while his 'Echoes' column for *Record Mirror* and—more recently—*Let It Rock* receives consistent praise. Twenty-eight years old, Millar intends to continue writing monographs on all aspects of vintage Rock 'n' Roll.

## ACKNOWLEDGEMENTS

I COULD not have written this book without the assistance of many friends and experts. The following list includes all the most generous contributors.

Among those I would particularly like to thank are Bob Galgano, who kindly supplied tapes of The Robins recorded output; Cliff White, who sacrificed his Coasters collection for the best part of a year; Kurt Mohr, for placing his invaluable Coasters discography at my disposal; Norbert Hess, for discographical assistance and permission to use rare illustrations; Dick Horlick, for sharing his unrivalled knowledge of black vocal groups and Ray Topping for help of kinds too various to specify. I am also grateful to the following, all of whom provided guidance or much needed information: John Ashworth, Colin Escott, Rob Finnis, Pete Grendysa, Rob Hughes, Ken Keating, Ken Major, John McIver, Steve Richards, Clive Richardson, Roy Stanton, Ron Weiser, and, not least, my editor, Mark Howell. As an insight collector of plagiarist proportions, I've been glad to read the work of Charlie Gillett, Rod Gruver, Michael Lydon, Paul Oliver, and Richard Williams. For historical reference, 'Billboard' and 'Cashbox' magazines were endlessly helpful and I am indebted to Terry Whittaker of Carlin Music and Thomas Levy of The Aberbach Group for their most sympathetic assistance with copyright problems. I have left till last my most important debt, to my wife, Marlene, who assisted in the preparation of the manuscript and learned more about The Coasters than she ever needed to know.

The author is very grateful to the following publishers for permission to quote from material in their copyright:

Progressive Music Publishing Co, Inc and Carlin Music Corporation Ltd, for 'Down in Mexico', 'One Kiss led to Another', 'Young Blood', 'Yakety Yak', 'Charlie Brown', 'Keep on Rollin', 'Stewball', 'Crazy Baby', 'What about Us', 'Three Cool Cats', 'Along Came Jones', 'Wake me, Shake Me', 'Poison Ivy', 'I'm a Hog for You', 'Ridin' Hood', 'Girls, Girls, Girls', 'Little Egypt', 'I can't hear a word you Say', 'Saved', 'You're the Boss', 'Your Old Lady', and 'The Climb'; Carlin Music Corporation Ltd, for 'Speedo's Back in Town'; Quintet Music Publishing Co and Carlin Music Corporation Ltd, for 'Riot in Cell Block No. 9', 'Framed', 'The Hatchet Man', 'Love Potion No. 9', 'Wrap it Up', 'If Teardrops were Kisses', 'I must be Dreamin' ', and 'Smokey Joe's Cafe'; Tiger Music Publishing Co and Carlin Music Corporation Ltd, for 'What is The Secret of your Success', 'Idol with the Golden Head', and 'Papa Daddy'; Trio Music Publishing Co and Carlin Music Corporation Ltd, for 'Everybody's Woman', 'Bull Tick Waltz', 'Soul Pad', 'Down Home Girl', and 'She Can'; Southern Music Publishing Co Ltd, for 'Stranded in the Jungle'; Lark Music Ltd, for 'Mainliner', 'Saturday Night Daddy', 'Kansas City', and 'Sixty Minute Man'.

## CONTENTS

CHAPTER ONE

# ROOTS

THIS book has three inextricably linked concerns: The Coasters, their predecessors The Robins, and their producers, Jerry Leiber and Mike Stoller. Their stories began in the late forties when rock 'n' roll was unknown and its tributaries, rhythm and blues and country and western, had not long been defined. At that time, mainstream popular music was dominated by six major record companies, Columbia, RCA-Victor, Decca, MGM, Capitol and Mercury. The 'majors' had dabbled heavily in blues before 1940 but, during World War II, they marked time and, as raw materials became scarce, they economized on all but the most obviously popular product.

On the other hand, rhythm and blues (initially called 'race' music and hereafter abbreviated to r & b) was beginning to grow, a phenomenon directly attributable to the great migration of potential black consumers from the depressed Southern states to the cities of the North and West in search of a better life. This new market was rapidly monopolized by small, independent labels whose owners recognized black music as an unexploited commodity. By the end of the forties, major companies found themselves out in the cold; r & b was now firmly established in the hands of the 'indies' of which King (in Cincinatti), Savoy, Jubilee (New Jersey), Atlantic (New York), Chess (Chicago), Modern, Aladdin, Specialty, and Imperial (all based in Los Angeles where armament factories had attracted many thousands of blacks from all over the South and Mid-West) were by far and away the most important.

The popularity of r & b placed increasing emphasis on record sales and by 1949 the weekly trade paper, *Billboard*, was listing r & b hits in a separate section to that of the best selling popular records. The two forms of music were diametrically opposed and, apart from the work of Louis Jordan (one of the very few blacks with a major label contract), both markets were utterly segregated. With the passing of big band swing in the mid-forties, popular music pursued a broad but uniformly bland spectrum of novelty songs, melodramatic ballads, and sentimental orchestrated themes. R & b was loud, noisy, and demonstrably exciting. It did not use the string then identified with mass appeal pop music and, unlike the latter, the lyrics of r & b songs were frequently concerned with the negative results of urban living—alcoholism, infidelity and crime. Musical integration is now an accepted fact. A r & b record that achieves widespread acceptance outside the Negro market may also be called a pop hit. Over twenty-five years ago, no r & b records became pop hits. Since the major companies controlled retail outlets, mass media promotion, and their own distribution networks, the indies were generally content to specialize in nothing but black music for black consumption. Unlike the majors who worked with entrenched musical forms along equally well-established principles, the independent label owner occupied an unscrupulous and briskly competitive world, one in which song writers sold their compositions for ten dollars, the word 'producer' was unheard of and where concern for the artist's well-being was very often the last consideration.

You are about to read how two Jewish teenagers from the North-East and a number of black singers from the South met up in Los Angeles and began to change that world beyond recognition. The path on which they embarked was fraught with obstacles but slowly and inexorably they eradicated the musical colour line. Few then realized that r & b would become so dominant a facet of Western culture and this book examines the very considerable part which Leiber and Stoller and The Coasters had to play in that enormous cultural growth.

Jerry Leiber and Mike Stoller were the first blue-eyed soul brothers, writing for a host of bluesmen from 1949 onwards. They were the first to bring satire and a social conscience to rock at a time when it was chiefly concerned with songs about a boy who just had to have a girl. They were also the first independent producers, ushering out the simplicity of an era in which records were made by pulling groups off the streets and into studios where they mouthed 'doo wop' and 'doo wah' into a microphone for three minutes. From these primitive beginnings to monaural overdubbing, the first eight-track studios, and on into the realms of the technological future shock, Leiber and Stoller have directed all the phases of post-war record production. They were largely responsible for transforming it into an art form as important as the music to which it relates and their influence as record producers has been drastic beyond measure.

In 1953 they began to develop an unusually adventurous method of recording black singers, using material they wrote themselves and enhancing the sound by employing hitherto unknown arrangements and studio techniques. With The Robins, they made a string of individual morality plays into which they distilled a neat and witty combination of guts and well-observed narrative. These records began to sell across racial barriers and formed the basis for their work with The Coasters for whom they perfected an overall concept, writing and producing as many as seventeen nationally popular hit records between 1955 and 1962. These little plastic works of art number some of the most innovative and influential records in rock's history.

While many black vocal groups had a greater number of hit records, none enjoyed such a long period of mass acceptance without some alteration to the basic ingredients of their style. Primarily, no other combination has so consistently resisted the self-consciousness brought about by popular success. They maintained their popularity without reflecting stylistic change; in 1969, fifteen years after the groups' creation, Nik Cohn was able to write: 'They're still around and occasionally a new single filters through. Nothing vital is changed . . . they live in a cut off private world and everyone is sweet sixteen for ever.'[1] The Coasters' records were also the white adolescent's introduction to the culture of the urban black; since they dealt almost exclusively with promiscuity, crime, and other failures, it could be argued that they helped to hide any culture he had. I have thought it right to devote some space to both sides of this controversial question. Those aspects of Leiber and Stoller's activities which directly concern both The Robins and The Coasters—their pioneering interest in r & b, the records they made with each and their eventual disenchantment with the recording industry—attracts most emphasis. That their involvement with other artists and media is dealt with only briefly is no indication that such work is of less importance; I simply hope to permit a more thorough study of The Coasters and, of course, their special relationship with Leiber and Stoller, than would otherwise be possible.

I have been extremely fortunate in obtaining interviews with most of the important participants. Dick Horlick spoke to Ty Terrell and Bobby Nunn while Ron Weiser talked to Richard Berry; both were kind enough to pass on the results of their vital research. I spoke to Johnny Otis when he toured Britain with his revue in July 1972. As many enthusiasts discovered, Johnny is the perfect interviewee willing to discuss the entire spectrum of r & b for hours on end. For guiding me through The Coasters prehistory I cannot thank him enough. Charlie Gillett kindly arranged an interview with Mike Stoller who was in London about the same time in order to produce Stealers Wheel. It was shorter than I would have wished but without Stoller's dryly amusing conversation the book would be nothing. To Mike Stoller then, a big thank you. I am equally grateful to Buck Ram and, of course, The Coasters—Cornel Gunter, Billy Guy, Earl Carroll, and especially

Carl Gardner for showing endless patience in the face of intolerable inquisitiveness. Finally, the song lyrics quoted herein have been transcribed from records without reference to other sources or ears and I apologize now for any inaccuracies that may have occurred.

* * *

The story of The Coasters really begins in San Francisco where, at Alameda High School in 1945, Ty Terrell met twin brothers, Billy and Roy Richards, and teamed up to form The 'A Sharp' Trio. Terrell, a tenor, and the Richards brothers, both baritones although Roy doubled as bass, were the fundamental core of a group which became known as The Robins. Their names are not familiar to all students of popular music and the many records they made (some eighty titles between 1947 and 1960) are often equally esoteric. They arrived however during the very emergence of rhythm and blues and it would not be useful to discuss their career outside this wide perspective. Their place in the confluence of styles which made Los Angeles the most important centre in the genesis of post-war r & b; their association with the major musical figures of the early r & b pantheon and the operations of the many small, independent companies for whom they recorded, more than justifies some attention to the groups' history. Described, by most of their musical associates, as a loose aggregation of modest talents, The Robins nonetheless loom large in the lives of numerous, more renowned names. Over seventeen years they were to add a variety of star singers—Bobby Nunn, Richard Berry, Carl Gardner—and to launch the careers of, among others, Little Esther Phillips, H. B. Barnum, Jerry Leiber and Mike Stoller, whose first recorded composition was by The Robins, and, of course, The Coasters to whom they gave birth in 1955.

Terrell, who was born near Jackson, Mississippi in 1930, moved to California in 1939. A mutual wish to become involved in the theatre led to the formation of The 'A Sharp' Trio who struck out for Hollywood in 1946. Until Hunter Hancock arrived on the airwaves with 'Harlem Matinee' the same year, Los Angeles had no black radio programmes and the Trio, none of whom had sung in church, were influenced entirely by popular juke-box records of the day; The Nat Cole Trio, The Andrews Sisters, and much older black groups, the Delta Rhythm Boys and the Golden Gate Quartet, were particularly favoured. At first, they aimed high, hanging around the Million Dollar Theatre—The Apollo of Los Angeles—where they tried to sell themselves to Stan Kenton, Floyd Ray, Lionel Hampton—indeed any of the large bands to perform on the big-time, swing band circuit. When common sense defeated youthful optimism, they headed for The Barrelhouse, a newly opened club in Watts, owned by Johnny Otis who ran a talent contest on Thursday evenings.

Popularly known as 'The Godfather of Rhythm and Blues', Otis is genetically white but black in every other conceivable respect. An integrated childhood and a life-long association with black musicians has meant that there have always been places where he couldn't dance, sleep, or eat and his autobiography, an uncompromising yet honest and thoroughly absorbing document called *Listen to The Lambs*,[2] reveals a devotion to blacks and their cause second to none. John Alexander Veliotes was born of Greek parents in Vallejo, California in 1921. He began playing drums for the Barrelhouse Blues Stompers in 1936 and toured Texas and Nebraska with the bands of Count Otis Matthews, George Morrison, and Lloyd Hunter until 1942 when he returned to California with Harlan Leonard's Kansas City Rockets and formed his own band at the Club Alabam in Los Angeles. At first they were unable to record: 'Previous to the Forties we had just three record companies, Decca, Victor, and Columbia and that's about it. An artist like Roy Milton or even myself couldn't play anywhere, Victor and Columbia weren't interested in us small fry. Somewhere along the line, The Rene brothers, Otis and Leon, fellows who had moved from New Orleans to L.A. said, "What the fuck do you need to be a record company? All you got to do is go get a record, get it pressed, and put it out. There are no special franchises involved?" So they started a record company—actually had two, Exclusive and Excelsior—and soon there were a whole bunch of independent labels here. Guys like The Renes and The Bihari brothers actually built pressing plants and, even though it was hard to get material during wartime, they got the wax and the shellac and whatever else it was and they put little bullshit records together. They couldn't get Basie or Duke, couldn't afford them. So what was left to them was T-Bone Walker, Joe Liggins, Roy Milton, Charles Brown, myself, Big Jay McNeely, things like that. They'd take people like ourselves into the studio and, for a couple of hundred bucks, the whole thing is done and the next day you actually have records.'[3]

Thus, in 1945, Otis began playing drums at sessions for Illinois Jacquet, Wynonie Harris, Johnny Moore's Three Blazers, Lester Young, and Timmie Rogers; Jacquet's 'Flying Home' (Aladdin 101) and Johnny Moore's 'Drifting Blues' (Aladdin 112), with a vocal by Charles Brown, were among the historic and hugely influential jazz and blues recordings to which the 24-year-old Otis lent his considerable expertise. The following year he recorded a wealth of material for Excelsior, including a successful big band version of 'Harlem Nocturne' (Excelsior 142), but it was a final fling. Thereafter the popularity of big bands sharply declined and Otis was forced to disband his 17 piece orchestra in favour of an eight piece combo. In doing so, he was among the pioneers who synthesised elements of pre-war country blues with big band instruments to create a new, hybrid music which was instantly popular with the proliferating independent record labels and their audience. Rhythm and blues was born, he recalls, out of economic necessity: 'We were forced into a small band situation but through my years with the big bands I'd realized that the thing that people really loved was what we loved too, the blues. We didn't need to get fancy just to do what comes naturally and effortlessly. It was the folk music with the driving beat and it differed from the old country thing because I just had to have some horns. We'd get a couple of saxes and a trumpet—we'd still have our horns but by coincidence it also made a very unique sound and I love it. I suddenly realized I didn't want four trumpets and five saxes, absolutely not. I wanted four horns with the baritone sticking out, that bluesy sound.'[4]

Synonymous with the rise of independent labels and local air-play, rhythm and blues boomed and Otis' club, The Barrelhouse, was packed solid, night after night: 'Suddenly here was a place where this revolutionary, new, loose, swinging, rocking, blues and rhythm could be heard.'[5] The 'A Sharp' Trio arrived at the Barrelhouse in 1947 and brushed up two numbers, a standard, 'Ooh Looka there, Ain't she pretty' and 'Satchelmouth Baby', a song previously recorded by the Basin Street Boys on the reverse of the then popular Leon Rene tune, 'I sold my heart to the Junkman'. They sang both and, according to Terrell, broke up the show. Otis gave them a weekend job, Friday, Saturday, and Sunday nights, for five dollars each and, later the same year, they made their first record, 'My Baby done told me', for Otis Rene's Excelsior label which described them as The Four Bluebirds; the name changed quickly. Johnny Otis, who was responsible for arranging the session, describes how The Robins were born: 'We had talent shows on Thursday nights and, one Thursday, a group came in calling themselves "A Sharp" Trio. I remember they came from Alameda because I was raised near-by in Berkeley, San Francisco. They sang and they won a prize. second prize I think because that same evening a young man walked in with a tiny amplifier and a raggedy little guitar and he won first prize and that was Pete Lewis. I immediately put him with the band and he stayed with me for years. But the Richards brothers and Terrell were animated and the people seemed to like them. I had a kid doing odd jobs around The Barrelhouse named Bobby Nunn. He was a friend of my drummer, Leard "Kansas City" Bell. Leard loved Joe Turner and he would get up and sing duets with Bobby who had a real deep voice like Ricky (Jimmy Ricks) of The Ravens. They went well together but when these three guys walked in and won a prize, it occurred to me that I oughta put Bobby Nunn with them so I'd have a group like The Ravens. So I added Bobby and called them The Four Bluebirds because The Orioles, The Larks—that trend had developed. As a matter of fact Bluebirds are very dark and—it's an interesting sociological point—might suggest a Blackbird and, in those days, that word was utterly taboo. They loathed the name because of the colour factor and members of my band soon put me wise so after the first record we changed it to The Robins.'

Bobby Nunn, a founder member of The Coasters, was born in Birmingham. Alabama, in 1925. Before joining the U.S.A.F., where he became welterweight boxing champion of the Pacific Fleet, he had sung as a member of an itinerant black revue, The Brownskin Models. Demobbed in Los Angeles in 1947, he had been persuaded to try his luck at the Barrelhouse where he appeared in a talent contest with Dallas Red. After a brief period stacking chairs, he joined Billy, Roy, and Ty with whom he stayed until 1955. The Robins made no further records for Excelsior but virtually lived in recording studios until they retired. In May 1949, Aladdin, owned by Eddie Mesner, released 'Around about Midnight' and 'You sure look good to me' on a subsidiary, score. Several months later, two songs from the same session, 'Don't like the way you're doing' and 'Come Back Baby', appeared on the parent label itself. 'Around about Midnight', originally issued only on 78 r.p.m., was made available in 1970 on 'Rhythm and Blues: Sweet and Greasy' LM 94005), an album in United Artists 'Legendary Master Series', lovingly compiled by Bob Hite and

Henry Vestine of the contemporary group, Canned Heat.

A recording of exceptional clarity, 'Around about Midnight' is a sophisticated city blues in the relaxed, introspective piano/guitar style of Johnny Moore's Three Blazers who, with their singer, Charles Brown, also recorded for Aladdin. White blues historians have long paid scant attention to the form, preferring the simpler, harsher, unvarnished music of performers from Mississippi or Chicago despite the fact that, as far as a national black audience was concerned, blues from Los Angeles enjoyed a popularity infinitely greater than any comparable locality. Charles Brown, with seven top ten r & b hits under his own name between 1949 and 1952, led the field but many others—Floyd Dixon, Pee Wee Crayton, Lowell Fulson, Little Willie Littlefield, Lloyd Glenn—enjoyed best-sellers in the same subdued and reflective vein. The other main city development, a far noisier rough-house combo sound popularized by Roy Milton and Joe and Jimmy Liggins, was also in favour while Amos Milburn, whose records often fell into either category, enjoyed even more hits than Charles Brown. Nonetheless, Brown's influence on both Johnny Otis and The Robins was virtually indelible; it was a style to which they returned again and again well into the fifties.

Bobby Nunn's urbane lead vocal (although born in Alabama he was raised in Detroit) was simply too much like Charles Brown to succeed and the Aladdin material was not commercially fortunate. The group continued to appear with the Johnny Otis show at the Barrelhouse and, towards the end of 1949, the entire revue was signed to Savoy, a Newark based label founded by Herman Lubinsky ten years before. Johnny Otis takes up the story: 'We were recommended to Lubinsky by Ralph Bass, a local talent scout cum a & r man for Savoy records in the East. Ralph came down the club and what he saw really excited him. Lubinsky flew out and persuaded me to sign. As they say in "The Godfather" he made me an offer I couldn't refuse. Not a gun to my head but in my case he enticed me with these words—"sign this contract son for one cent and if you give me one hit record, I'll triple it". I gave that mother fucker eight hits and he hasn't even doubled it.' In a world of hustlers, it is impossible to establish the veracity of a claim such as this, although Otis would undoubtedly have plenty of supporters for his point of view.

Ralph Bass, a white New Yorker, had travelled to Los Angeles during the Depression. His love of black music had led to jobs with several of the new independent race labels including Black and White where he produced his first hit, Jack McVea's 'Open The Door Richard' (792), in 1947. He travelled on the road with most of the acts he was responsible for recording including the Otis revue. With Bass in charge The Robins cut at least eleven songs for Savoy in four separate sessions. Each was held at Radio Recorders on Santa Monica. 'In the whole of L,A,' said Otis, 'there were only a couple of people who were able to engineer this music and do it to our satisfaction. Bunny Robyn over on Fairfax Avenue was one and the other was Val Valentine at Radio Recorders. Val, a man of Puerto Rican origin, now heads the Verve organization but then he had the best equipped studios to my knowledge. It was a fine place and, more important, he understood when we wanted a twangy guitar. Now we know about equalization, we've learnt. Back then, however, all we knew was what we wanted to hear. The engineer would make the drum prominent and slap the afterbeat for us or he wouldn't. Usually they'd refuse, they didn't like the idea, it wasn't up to standard, they thought it was distorted. We were after that very twangy loose guitar and that cracking drum and there were times we tried other studios and left in despair. Most engineers were a very snobbish lot in those days because they were used to recording Jack Benny, Bing Crosby whoever and we'd come in. We were black and we had these raggedy little instruments and we presumed to tell them what we wanted and it turned out disastrously. Val, knew exactly what we were after and we used Radio Recorders for several years. I produced the Savoy things there although I didn't know it because someone else was getting the fee. Roy Milton, Charles Brown, Joe Liggins—we all produced ourselves but we didn't know the meaning of the word. The "proper" producer just stood by as a supervisor for technical reasons. There was no multi-track recording, just mono and studio time was so short we'd completely rehearse The Robins before we got there. Lubinsky was a slave driver, he wanted a session in exactly three hours and he'd threaten us with not releasing the record if we went into overtime. We were dumb enough to believe every word. I had a little chicken ranch out in Watts and we'd rehearse there or at The Barrelhouse so by the time we got to the studio it was ready; one or two takes and the whole thing was finished.'

Beyond an increasingly large number of white collectors (whose tastes are influenced more by a record's rarity than by such variables as musical quality) the sides which The Robins made for Savoy have a severely limited appeal. As a body of recordings they have not stood the test of time; like flies in amber they are indubitably fixed to the moment in which they were created. While this is very often true of records made by most black harmony groups, those by The Robins seem particularly fossilized. Their subdued mournful, after-hours quality continued to have much in common with the low-key urban blues of solo performers like Charles Brown and very little of the gospel influence apparent in groups like The Ravens, The Dominoes, The Flames, or The Swallows who also featured a bass or baritone lead. The format, popular with black audiences during the late forties and early fifties, did not survive among the stylistic changes which overtook the first black groups to enjoy bi-racial appeal. Then the role of the bass singer quickly became that of comedian and his contribution—he was rarely permitted to sing an entire song—existed largely for novel effect. There was nothing intentionally funny about Bobby Nunn's first work with The Robins—his exceptionally narrow range was less melodious than either Bill Brown (of The Dominoes) or Jimmy Ricks (of The Ravens) and, as Johnny Otis has constantly remarked, The Richards brothers were very often 'slightly out of tune'.

'Some guy,' said Otis, 'Someone with a tin ear, like some of the collectors who think that vocal groups were the last word, might refer to things like "Our Romance is Gone" as the *avant garde* of the day but it's really not that, it's wrong notes some of The Robins are singing there. It's too bad the vocals are in there, it would be a nice instrumental, Pete Lewis is playing so fine.'

'You know,' Otis continued, 'there's no blanket condemnation on my part of vocal groups. Why on the East Coast they have such nice harmonies. Musically and artistically, I love The Drifters, the Moonglows, The Clovers, they were great. But even my dear friends like The Penguins, The Medallions, and those other West Coast sounds were horrible. I used to talk to my bass man and my trumpet player and we used to say, "there must be something here in the water that causes that." I mean listen to The Robins creating a whole new world of music, a new principle of harmonics called "wrong notes".'

To compensate for these deficiencies, musical accompaniment—barely noticeable in records by many of the groups' contemporaries—was frequently emphatic. Vibes, played by Johnny Otis, have the curiously old fashioned effect of clinking milk bottles while the other members of his quintet—Devonia 'Lady Dee' Williams (piano), Pete Lewis (guitar), Mario Delagarde (bass), and Leard Bell (drums)—supplied a robust and often inventive support. Lewis was an extraordinarily good guitarist given to melodic improvisation but more often required to thrash huge blocks of muddy chords from his instrument whenever the vocal performance appeared to grind to a halt.

The Robins' first session produced one of their better ballads, 'There's Rain in my Eyes'. Their personalities do not leap out of the grooves but no one sings flat and, as a whole, it is probably the least cobwebbed selection. Collectors of musical curiosa will be intrigued to hear Otis' recollections: 'There was a performer who worked at The Barrelhouse with us, a little song and dance man who'd enjoyed some prominence in the minstrel shows of the twenties. He brought me the song which he said he'd written and it was infinitely superior to anything I'd written for The Robins. I enthused and he said, "Right, I give you permission to record it." After we did the session, someone tipped us off by bringing the sheet-music in. It had come out in the thirties written by Oscar Hammerstein or some such and there it was, "Rain in my Eyes" by Ray Noble and his Band. Bardu Ali, my partner, got the little bastard when he came to work. Bardu had a cap pistol and, while I started talking to the guy, he turned round and Bardu had the gun in one hand and the sheet music in the other. The guy started sweating and lying, it was the greatest reaction. The first discs came out with his name on them, but eventually we had to change the credits.'

The second session, in December 1949, provided Otis with two of his eight hits and gave black record buyers a national anthem. 'Double Crossing Blues', which featured The Robins harmonizing behind a duet between Bobby Nunn and the then unknown Little Esther, topped the r & b charts and remained among the best-sellers for six months. Universally known as Esther Phillips—she took the surname from a hoarding over a gas station when making a comeback with 'Release Me' (Lenox 5555) in 1962—Esther May Jones was born in Galveston, Texas on 23 December 1935. She was soon addicted to rhythm and blues: 'I learnt all my early singing in church but around the age of nine I started listening to records by Charles Brown, Amos Milburn, and Dinah Washington. At that time Dinah was really my only favourite, I would save my milk money and stop and play her records on the way home from school.'[6] She travelled to Los Angeles with her family in 1948 and, shortly thereafter, her sister entered her for a talent contest at the Largo Theatre. Johnny Otis was in the audience and he enjoys talking of the events which led to Esther's discovery, the enormous success of 'Double Crossing Blues' and the atmosphere in which the record was made:

'There were two theatres in Watts. One black and one Mexican that played Spanish shows. The Largo was closest to The Barrelhouse, about eight blocks away. Late in '49 I cut my fingers and the first night out of hospital I went to the Largo theatre with Big Jay McNeely—Cecil McNeely he was then—and my bass player, Mario Delagarde. Things were occurring on stage, there were three people who were later in varying degrees of prominence, Esther at the top of the heap, Mickey Champion and another girl who became a semi-name. Big Jay played his horn behind two of the girls and they were really good. Then they came to this little girl and she started singing a Dinah Washington song, "Baby get lost", and it was really beautiful. I turned to Mario, "Jesus Christ that's great, a young kid like that, she's wonderful." A girl sitting right in front of me turned around and said, "That's my sister." I said "Well, go get her baby," and that was that. The following Thursday, Esther won first prize at The Barrelhouse but right then I didn't know what I was going to do with her. Nothing had been planned and "Double Crossing Blues" was a happy accident to begin with. I had a feeling I could emulate The Ravens with The Robins because of Bobby Nunn's bass voice and that I had another Dinah Washington in Little Esther because that's exactly who she idolized. I thought I'd just see if we couldn't get a song where we could put them together. Jessie Mae Robinson had submitted a song to me called "What's a matter Baby", a little blues song with about four verses. I'd also written an untitled song which was based on an old comedy act, Apus and Estralita, which I'd seen years ago in vaudeville. They were a black man and woman who had a song and dance thing, very funny. In the middle of their act, she'd say to him—she was very attractive and he was a very homely dude—"You should be out in the forest fightin' a grizzly bear," and he would say, "How come you ain't out. . . .' and she'd butt in with "I'm a lady," and he'd say, "Hell, they got lady bears out there," and the audience would crack up see. So I started to write a song. I forget how it went but I had two verses including that catchphrase. My eyes fell right on Jessie Mae's song lying on my bed and thought I Jeez if I took those two verses and tagged them on we'd have a great song. Hers started out "Been lookin' for you baby" and worked right into the break choruses I had written. I called Jessie and she said "Go ahead, we'll be collaborators."

'Then one morning in November, I was leaving the chicken ranch—118th and Wilmington—to take The Robins to Radio Recorders and Esther came running up hollering "Wait for me." We'd never rehearsed the song with her but we got through four sides with The Robins and we ended up twenty minutes early. I turned to Ralph Bass and said, "Let me take this twenty minutes." He said, "Aw we got enough already, forget it." I persisted. "No, I gotta little thing here, I want you to listen to it." He gave in, so we rehearsed it with Esther and there was three minutes left. We did one take but Esther giggled during the song. I said, "One more take, Ralph," but he refused. I argued, "But she giggled, Ralph we gotta do it again." He said, "Nope, it's too bad, we'll have to go into overtime." It was a shambles 'cos not only that, I'd just come out of hospital, my right arm was in a cast and I was playing the vibes with my left hand. I begged him to let us do it again but he shrugged me off, "Aw, it's not going anywhere, anyhow." He sent little dubs of the session to Lubinsky back East. Lubinsky played it and thought it was a cheap imitation of The Ravens and Dinah Washington and wasn't going to release it. A guy named Bill Cook, a dee-jay in New Jersey, dropped by Lubinsky's office just after the tapes arrived. Lubinsky gave him The Robins stuff and Bill seized this one-sided thing, "What's this?" Lubinsky said, "Ah some shit that Johnny Otis sent out here." Bill told me later that's exactly what he said. Well he played "Double Crossing Blues" over the air that night and it became a big hit. It was a colossal break but things went wrong right away.

'The song was a succcess because of the line I had lifted from Apus and Estralita and what Jessie Mae had written could have been anything, it could have been instrumental and it would still have made it. I gave her correct credit and I felt a handshake between friends was O.K. I couldn't believe what she did, she seemed such a mild, sweet person. She had signed with Hill and Range as a writer and told them the situation and they said, "Well, we'll take the whole song" and they did. Lubinsky talked me out of fighting it and again, out of ignorance, I allowed them to get away with it—pity, aside from the money, I felt a little proud artistically because it had a nice feeling to it.

*'What's a matter daddy, don't my kisses satisfy,*
*If I don't thrill you baby, goodness knows how hard I try!'*

It was undeniably strong stuff coming from a 13-year-old but Little Esther, who imitates every felicitous trick in Dinah Washington's book, sang with a plaintive maturity.

The song is likely to have sold an unprecedented 400,000 copies. It was pressed over and over again appearing with two different flip-sides, 'Nothin' Shakin''—an institutional catch phrase in the black community—by Leon Sims and 'Back Alley Blues', an instrumental by The Beale Street Boys. Neither involved Johnny Otis or The Robins, and Otis has a very strong, though personal, opinion on this: 'That's because Herman Lubinsky is a thief. I don't say this about all the men I've worked for—I love The Biharis and The Mesners as deep, personal friends but not Lubinsky because he was a congenital rogue. He wouldn't have to pay me for the other side, it was an immoral thing to do to us but he didn't even pay me for the top side so what's the difference.'

'If it's so Baby' and 'If I didn't love you so', another

coupling from the 'Double Crossing' session, were issued a month earlier in December 1949. 'If it's so Baby' made a fleeting appearance on the r & b chart the following February but it was soon eclipsed by 'Double Crossing Blues' and no other Robins records for Savoy were even remotely successful. In 1950 they made another four songs with the Otis Quintette including 'Ain't no use Beggin'', a bass-tenor duet and, perhaps the best—it had two solos from Pete Lewis—an untempo booter, 'I'm living O.K.' Although sought after now 'Double Crossing Blues' was still high on the charts and they did not sell then. 'Sometimes the American audience can be complimented,' said Otis, 'they rejected those things out of hand.'

Johnny Otis, however, became Savoy's most valuable asset riddling the best-selling lists with a succession of hits with Little Esther, Mel Walker, and those by his own band. His was the first, biggest and most celebrated caravan of stars to hit the road. Atlantic's Joe Morris covered the East (with Billy Mitchell, Jimmy Lewis, and Little Laurie Tate as the counterpart to Little Esther) but he could not approach Otis who simply monopolized the r & b chart with six smash hits—all top fifteen—in 1950 alone. While the first of these—'If it's so Baby' and 'Double Crossing Blues' —were popularized by The Robins, the glory which was soon reflected on the Otis troupe did not extend to them. The Robins and Otis parted company less than amicably. '"Double Crossing Blues" was really huge,' Otis recalls, 'We began feeling these waves in L.A. and it spread right through the black community, not the pop market of course, it was strictly a race hit. One day I was summoned to an office downtown, I can't recall the cat's name (Ralph Bass remembered that it was Ed Fishman), but he was an agent. The Robins were sitting round and he sat me down and told me that they were the most important thing on the record—Esther was just window dressing—and that he was gonna set up a national tour. Esther would be hired as an employee and if I'd like to go along as a musical director for twenty dollars a night I'd be welcome. I sacked Bobby Nunn's arse, dropped the slightly out-of-tune Robins and used members of the band for back-up vocals.'

Mario Delagarde, Pete Lewis, and two saxophonists, Lorenzo Holden and Walter Henry became The Jayos for vocal purposes. The arrangement, like many of the events described in this first chapter, took place well over twenty years before the main participants were interviewed. When human recollection fails, imagination often takes its place. There may have come a time when the imagination of one participant competed with another in recounting incidents of which there can be no entirely accurate recollection. Yet differing narratives are often delivered with equal confidence and it is therefore right to include both sides to each controversial question. While Otis claims not to have billed his musicians as The Robins, Ty Terrell remembers the circumstances rather differently: '"Double Crossing Blues" caught on all around the country. Someone showed me a "Cashbox" and I see it had sold something like 30,000 copies in three days. While this was going on we recorded other things and also backed up Little Esther and Mel Walker but they didn't put our names on the label. We got fifteen dollars for each record and we were tired of getting no credit. There was some sort of conspiracy, Johnny and Ralph Bass were arranging this tour but me and the Richards brothers got left out and Melvin Lightsey—they changed his name to Mel Walker—took Bobby Nunn's place while they used guys out of the band and called them The Robins. It was one of the first disappointments we had. "Double Crossing Blues" was burning it up all around the nation and whenever we'd see anyone important we'd say we just got back off tour but in fact we never even left town."[7]

Late in 1950, The Robins secured a fresh engagement at Billy Byrd's night-club and recorded a song called 'That's What the Good Book says' for Modern. It was a Jerry Leiber–Mike Stoller composition and, according to Leiber,

'It was a kind of fucked-up version of a blues and a gospel number and really not much of either. It was a pretty bad song but the first record we ever got.'[8] Three years elapsed before their paths crossed again and 'In the meantime,' said Terrell, 'we were recording for everybody in town. Each company would give you an exclusive contract and then you wouldn't hear any more. You wouldn't know whether they were gonna release the record or not. They paid you for the session, which would be about five dollars per person and that was the end of it, we never got a royalty statement in our lives. The Bihari boys had Modern and The Mesners had Aladdin and we'd go back and forth and in between we'd do things for Big John Dolphin who owned Recorded in Hollywood.'[9] Nunn agreed: 'Every time I looked around, someone wanted me to cut a record. Most of the time I didn't even sign my name.'[10] Such casual yet almost frenzied activity, common among groups during the early fifties, provides a rich tangle of material to unravel. Some mystery still surrounds the release, in 1950 and 1951, of titles on RPM by a group called the Nic-Nacs. Three sides, 'Found me a Sugar Daddy', 'Gonna have a Merry Christmas', and 'You didn't want my love', feature Little Esther and Bobby Nunn as well as The Robins. While contracted to Savoy they had simply moonlighted to RPM, a subsidiary of Modern, where their pseudonym may have fooled Herman Lubinsky if no one else. 'Found me a Sugar Daddy', released in December 1950, was, in fact, a skit on 'Double Crossing Blues':

*'I found me a sugar daddy, he looks just like a bear*
*His hair is short and nappy and he ain't goin' nowhere*
*He says he loves me, says my kisses satisfy*
*Well the way that man loves me, makes me feel good down inside.'*

'Gonna have a Merry Christmas' was equally gritty and it bears a fascinating resemblance to 'Santa Claus in Back in Town' which Leiber and Stoller wrote for Elvis Presley in 1957. It contains at least one double entendre which Presley—unlike Bobby Nunn—would not have been allowed to sing:

*'Now you can take down your stockings,*
*Turn out the Christmas light*
*I don't want no Santa Claus*
*Around my house on Christmas night.'*

On 8 December 1951, *Billboard* reported that Nunn had been signed by Dootsie Williams, a black orchestra leader whose newly founded Dootone label was another of the many (some 300 during the fifties) Los Angeles independents to rely almost exclusively on local black talent. Apart from 'Anticipation Blues' (Dootone 302), made with pianist Pete Johnson, Williams supervised two other sessions by Nunn. He leased the tapes to Blue, a subsidiary of MGM but no one I know has heard the titles which included 'I got a country Girl' (105) and 'Clappin' and Shoutin'' (115). The rarity of these is matched by The Robins next move, to Recorded in Hollywood and Big John Dolphin whose slogan, said Terrell, was 'We'll record you today and have you a hit tonight.' His first attempt—'Race of Man' c & w 'Bayou Baby Blues'—may well have sold fewer copies than any record made. Like a rare species of moth, a copy was discovered as late as 1970. Credited to The Robins and Two Sharps and a Natural, it was, recalled Nunn, 'cut in about an hour and a half. It's me singing on "Race of Man" which was an unusual sound because you had a mixture of white and black. I knew the two white boys who had written the song and we put them in there singing background behind The Robins. And that's Maggie Hathaway, the wife of band-leader Floyd Ray, singing lead like Little Esther on "Bayou Baby Blues". She told Dolphin she wanted to make a record with us behind her.'

A second record by The Robins 'Schoolgirl Blues' c & w 'Early Morning Blues', failed just as miserably and although Maggie Hathaway and Bobby Nunn made further solo sides for Recorded in Hollywood—'When Gabriel Blows His Horn (121) and 'Christmas Bells' (244) respectively—Dolphin did not record the group again. During the first half of 1952, Nunn was recalled into the armed forces and the group became inactive. Demobbed for the second time, Nunn quickly consolidated his position as the city's number one bass singer. He joined Little Esther for further records on Federal and rejoined The Robins who were signed to a major company, RCA-Victor. Both events led to a closer involvement with Jerry Leiber and Mike Stoller.

* * *

Born in Baltimore on 25 April 1933, Jerry Leiber moved to Los Angeles where he attended Fairfax High School in 1945. Three years later, Mike Stoller moved from New York to California; after one high school semester, he enrolled at Los Angeles City College. About 17 years old (Stoller may have been a year or two older than Jerry), both youths were keen blues fans.

Jerry Leiber: 'I'd say that I was influenced greatly in the forties by the people in the neighbourhood that I grew up in. I was brought up in a black and white neighbourhood and most of the black people had come up from the South to work in various plants and I was constantly exposed to blues and country music—that's the music and the poetry that had the greatest influence on me. I hadn't planned that early in life to write songs—that came later—not much later. I went out to California when I was twelve and I started writing songs when I was about sixteen. All the lyrics came out of eight and twelve bar blues. I was looking for a partner who could write music and someone told me about a very talented young man at City College and I was put in touch with him.'[11] The story is amplified by Mike Stoller: 'I got a call from Jerry who said he'd got my name from a friend of his who'd heard that I could write notes on paper. I said, "So what?" He said, "Well I'm writing songs" —he was very matter-of-fact, businesslike. I said, "Well I don't really like songs"—which was true and I also threw in a couple of references to Stravinsky. But he was persistent, said I'd like to meet you. Anyway he came to the house and I opened the door and just looked at him for a while—he had fiery red hair and one blue eye and one brown eye. After about three months of just standing there I said, "Come on in." He showed me the lyrics he had written in his school-book, I could see from the ditto lines under the first lines of most verses that a lot of them were blues. When he said song-writing I had thought he meant something else. I had always liked the blues and boogie-woogie piano since I was a kid. My idols were Pinetop Smith, Albert Ammons, Meade Lux Lewis and I used to play a kind of blues piano.'[12]

Leiber worked at a record store on Fairfax Avenue but also listened to blues in Dolphin's store on Central Avenue where he bumped into Lester Sill, then employed as a promotion man for Modern records. Sill would visit the premises where he would throw a pocketful of sand on the floor and do a shuffle dance to demonstrate the excitement of the Bihari brothers' new releases. Sill heard Leiber singing in the store and got around to talking about blues and songwriters. He fixed an appointment with The Biharis and Leiber and Stoller duly turned up. Stoller: 'We sat there for half an hour and whichever Bihari it was didn't show, we got very upset and walked down the street into Aladdin records. We went in there and they bought a couple of our songs.' Stoller's recollection fails to explain why Jerry Leiber credited The Robins' 'That's what the Good Book says' for Modern as the first of their songs to be recorded. Nonetheless, Leiber and Stoller had little difficulty in placing their earliest collaborations. Frank Bull and Gene Norman, then a prominent disc jockey, held a Blues Jubilee concert in Los Angeles during July 1951 and Norman gave them the names and addresses of all the performers who were scheduled to appear. Leiber and Stoller toured the Central Avenue district visiting each of the artists who included Wynonie Harris, Helen Humes, Floyd Dixon, Amos Milburn, Jimmy Witherspoon, and Charles Brown. Witherspoon accepted 'Real Ugly Woman' (Modern 821) while Floyd Dixon used 'Too much Jelly Roll' (Aladdin 3111), both of which were recorded live at Norman's Blues Jamboree. Several months later, Charles Brown cut 'Hard times' (Aladdin 3116) which, said Leiber, was considered a hit: 'It was the first hit we had and it sold 80,000 copies nationally. We were overjoyed because a hit at that time, a rhythm and blues hit, was 100,000. That was considered a very big hit. If you look at an old trade paper of the fifties you'll see that the territories are broken up. There was a pop hit parade, there was a c & w hit parade and there was a rhythm and blues hit parade. Now I know the same thing exists today but the overlap is great. In those days Charles Brown with a hit that sold 80,000 copies would be listed in Chicago Southside, Harlem, South Philly, New Orleans—the rhythm and blues tree. A regional listing—never a national listing.'[13]

In fact, 'Hard Times', which was bigger than Leiber remembered, made the national r & b top ten for three weeks in February 1952. Thereafter, Leiber and Stoller's compositions were snapped up as fast as they were written. Within a couple of years, their songs had been recorded by as many as twenty mainly local bluesmen including Roy Hawkins, Peppermint Harris, Bullmoose Jackson, Amos Milburn, Lucky Millinder, Big John Greet, Milt Trenier and his Solid Six, Preston Love, and Mel Walker. About this time Jerry Leiber and Lester Still drove all the way from Los Angeles to New York in order to meet Ralph Bass who had switched jobs from a & r at Savoy to a & r at King records, owned by Syd Nathan. A subsidiary label, Federal, had been launched in 1950 and, as it gathered steam, Bass leaned on Leiber and Stoller for material. 'He would call us up,' said Stoller, 'and say he had a session fixed for a singer, could we get to the studio with four songs. Sometimes we'd come with three and sit down and write the fourth while one of the others was being recorded.' Gradually, their contribution to these sessions increased: 'There were no lead sheets so we'd have to teach the singer the song and tell the band how the song was supposed to go. In effect, we began to do a production job, although of course we weren't being paid in that capacity.'

Among the many songs they wrote for Federal artists, there were two—'Mainliner', vocal by Little Esther and 'Saturday Night Daddy', a duet between Esther and Bobby Nunn (both Federal 12100)—on which Johnny Otis claims to have collaborated. While his band supplied the accompaniment, the composer credits list only 'Stroller (*sic*)–Leiber'. Recorded on 25 July 1952, both songs are worthy of comment. An unutterably funky introduction of deep train whistle, boogie piano and shouts of 'Mainline Baby' leads into a humourous sexual analogy which has nothing to do with injecting heroin as the title might suggest:

*'Let me be your sidetrack baby 'till your main line comes along*
*I'll steer you right daddy and I won't do you no wrong.*
*Come on daddy, let's have some fun*
*I can do better switches than your main line ever done*
*So go easy daddy, easy and slow*
*You can ride this track 'til you hear the whistle blow'*

The flip is a slower but equally sardonic blues duet:

Esther: *'Yes I got a daddy, finest man you've ever seen,*
*He's my Saturday Night Daddy 'cos he's married six days in between.'*
Nunn: *'Well pretty baby, it's a heck of a life,*
*One night of pleasure and then six more with my wife.'*

Needless to say, white radio stations would not accept records which celebrated adulterous sex (particularly with a young girl—Esther was still only sixteen years old) and it may well have been too risky even for black dee-jays. Neither side made the r & b charts which was unusual for Little Esther who had enjoyed seven top ten r & b hits in a row.

Performers were, as we have seen, either cunning or naïve, flitting from label to label under various pseudonyms. Independent record owners could be worse; rough and rugged pioneers, many were given to unscrupulous methods of business. This, and the mimeographed scraps of paper which frequently served as recording contracts, soon gave rise to a series of litigious squabbles which dominated the trade papers throughout the early fifties. When Little Esther sued Savoy over under-nourished royalties in May 1951, Lubinsky replied with a counter-claim alleging that her reputation was made via her Savoy recordings and at considerable expense and effort to the label. He also sought $50,000 in damages claiming that her unauthorized switch from Savoy to Federal had an adverse effect on Savoy's unreleased masters. In July the following year Lubinsky was sued by Sammy Lane, whose International label had signed Bobby Nunn in 1949, but Lubinsky won the case on the ground that Lane's one-year contract applied to the solo artist whereas he had signed Nunn and The Robins as a group.

Leiber and Stoller were caught up in a copyright controversy which persisted for several years.

In August 1952, Willie Mae 'Big Mama' Thornton recorded 'Hound Dog' (Peacock 1612), a stomping, rocking blues with a guttural vocal and excellent support from the Otis rhythm section including Pete Lewis who provides a really tough guitar solo. It was a giant smash, a number one on the r & b chart where it remained for over three months. It sold, according to Leiber, 'half a million records which was phenomenal at the time'.[14] Virtually all concerned promptly claimed a share of the song-writing credits. Willie Mae Thornton: 'Leiber and Stoller were a couple of kids then and they had this song written on the back of a brown paper bag. I started to sing the words and put in some of my own, all that talkin' and hollerin'—that's my own.'[15] Johnny Otis is more acrimonious: 'I was really taken to the cleaners on that "Hound Dog" thing because we had a working arrangement where Leiber and Stoller would bring the songs and I would edit them, make a contribution or occasionally re-write them. The agreement was that we would be co-writers as a result but when the big one finally came along they disaffirmed the contract through a technicality, by claiming they were minors or something, and cut me out. I'm not cynical about their talent—I admire them enormously—but I'm very bitter about that.'

The song first stirred up legal interest when Don Robey, owner of Peacock and its publishing affiliate, Lion Music, sued Sun records on the grounds that 'Bearcat' by Rufus Thomas (Sun 181)—a number three r & b hit in April 1953—had infringed their copyright. While the practice of cutting r & b 'answer' discs was common enough, the U.S. District Court ruled that 'Bearcat' was an infringement of 'Hound Dog' and Sun agreed to pay Robey two cents per record on all those sold. By July 1953, Little Esther had recorded a cover of 'Hound Dog' (Federal 12126) and Syd Nathan demanded 50 per cent of the publisher's share on the basis that Johnny Otis was under exclusive contract to Valjo, King's publishing branch, when he wrote the tune in collaboration with others. By 1956, when the song was revived as an eight-million seller by Elvis Presley (RCA 6604), Leiber and Stoller had re-established their claim to the entire composing credits. They remain unmoved by all other claims. Mike Stoller: 'Willie Mae would like to say she helped write "Hound Dog" but she didn't. Jerry and I wrote it but Johnny said he knew who could record it so he would take 50 per cent of the publishing. When it was first released Johnny was credited as a composer but we took the matter to court and we won in court, justly, because he had not been a writer so his name didn't appear on further records. We disaffirmed the contract it's true but this was simply because he didn't write it. He had asked us for a third of our end of the song which we agreed to on a certain basis but the basis was not complied with. We were all to co-publish the song—that was the agreement and Johnny was cut in on it. We formed a firm to publish the song and then unilaterally he signed the song to Don Robey's firm and indicated to Don that he had the right to sign for us which was all complete nonsense. Johnny, who I have really fond memories of, was often making three deals at once of an exclusive nature on the same sort of thing.'

On 18 August, a week after 'Hound Dog' was recorded, Leiber and Stoller scored again. Ralph Bass required more songs for a session he had arranged with Little Willie Littlefield, a popular singer/pianist with a slew of cheerful blues and boogies on Modern. They arrived with four: 'Striking on you baby' c & w 'Blood is Redder than Wine' (Federal 12101) and 'K.C. Loving' c & w 'Pleading at Midnight' (Federal 12110). Mike Stoller: 'Now we produced all those songs without any credit and with no royalty for production because there was no such thing, the word didn't really exist. The a & r man was a company employee and he really depended on us and the bandleader who was Maxwell Davis. We were only in the studio to protect our songs and to make sure that they got done right. In the case of "K.C. Lovin'" we went to Maxwell Davis' house and played the song to him and he wrote the arrangement for the band. Little Willie was there and he learned the song from Jerry and myself':

*'I'm goin' to Kansas City, Kansas City here I come* x 2
*They gotta crazy way of lovin' there an' I'm gonna get me some*
*I'm gonna be standin' on the corner, Twelfth Street and Vine* x 2
*With my Kansas City baby and a bottle of Kansas City wine.'*

Littlefield sold 100,000 copies in 1952 and a few more in 1959 when it was reissued as 'Kansas City' (Federal 12351) to compete with the million-seller by Wilbert Harrison (Fury 1023) who had remembered the words of the blues from the original recording. At Savoy, Bass had been paid sixty dollars a week; at King/Federal he obtained a percentage production deal and a publishing company which included the copyright to 'Kansas City'. 'Leiber and Stoller,' said Bass, 'were just two kids and I wanted to sign them as exclusive writers but Syd Nathan told me, "They'll never write another friggin' line." They were good kids; Mike was a serious cat, Lee was a real hot shot.'[16]

In 1953, Leiber and Stoller met up with The Robins whose manager, Chuck Landis, had pulled off a coup by obtaining a record contract with RCA-Victor earlier in the year. It was the first occasion either Leiber and Stoller or the group had worked with a major label. For The Robins it was also the last. 'They were not a new group,' said Stoller, 'Early in 1951—I have a pedantic memory for dates —they had recorded one song of ours, "That's What the Good Book says". But we didn't produce either side and the other side, "Rockin'", was nothing to do with us. In fact, The Biharis had a name called Taub which they added to any song just as a matter of course, whether or not they wrote it or had any right to it. We could give them a song as "Leiber and Stoller" and it would come out as "Leiber, Stoller, and Taub" automatically because someone in the office was told "Taub" goes on everything—it goes on every song just in case there's money there. (When asked who "Taub" was, Jules Bihari replied, "You're looking at him. The name comes from my mother." As far as actual earnings went it didn't mean anything.) Anyway, a buddy of ours, Jack Lewis, got us the job at Victor. He used to work in a record store in Los Angeles but he was then a & r man at RCA. He asked us to come in and kinda be, in effect, producers for The Robins. The Richards brothers and Ty Terrell were, like, the centre of the group along with Bobby

Nunn but they had various people who came in and dropped out because of armed service or armed robbery—they were either serving time or doing time. One of these guys was Grady Chapman who had a very high piercing voice.'

The Robins made ten sides for RCA-Victor and most were a marked improvement on any yet recorded by them. Nunn shared lead vocals with Grady Chapman and their repertoire was evenly divided between fast, riffy songs with horns and slow, polished Tin Pan Alley ballads with a muted rhythm section. These—'My Heart's the Biggest Fool', 'How would you know'—keep truly to the well-trodden path of other 'bird' groups like The Ravens and The Orioles. Just as the tenor and baritone swopped verses on several of the latter's biggest hits, so Nunn and Chapman sang duets like, 'Oh Why' and 'A Fool such as I', a dramatic version which may well have prompted the revival by Elvis Presley (RCA 7506) in 1959. 'Let's go to The Dance', a primitive but felicitous chant akin to the work of The Treniers, and 'Empty Bottles', a hot recital of alcoholic drinks from Pink champagne to Sneaky Pete, also deserve a wider hearing.

The r & b market was fast becoming surfeit with drink lyrics and Bobby Nunn, who eventually left The Coasters to avoid a duodenal ulcer, has explained why the subject was so popular a theme on black group records: 'Groups used alcohol heavily, not marijuana but mostly wine. Go backstage then and you would find everybody had scotch. At first we'd go and buy a whole gallon of wine and mix it with Seven Up. White port and Seven Up with a few ice cubes tastes like champagne. As you move on up, you start to drink whisky and it gets to be a habit but, no matter how drunk you got, you still knew exactly what you were gonna do onstage.'

The Robins were now making indubitably good records whose appeal ought to exceed those fortunate enough to possess the original 45's. The best of the lot was 'Ten Days in Jail'. 'Grady,' said Mike Stoller, 'could sing in a natural voice what most people had to do falsetto and he was the lead on "Ten Days in Jail" which we wrote and directed. Jack Lewis called out the take numbers and Shorty Rogers was the band on that.' It also has the distinction of being Leiber and Stoller's first prison song, a genre which they dipped into frequently in the years to come:

*'I got busted, poor poor me*
*I shouldna trusted Mary Lee*
*She set my name up, it was a frame-up*
*Somebody save me, warden gave me*
*Ten Days in Jail'*

The bouncy harmony phrases are catchy and the record actually swings. There is also the first germination of one of Leiber and Stoller's stock production devices when, during the final line of the refrain, Nunn's deep brown bass voice echoes Grady Chapman's shout of 'warden':

*'I don't dig this bread and water*
*I like my dinner made to order*
*I'm sittin' here bad as I could be*
*Warden (Warden) set me free.'*

It was a contrivance which would soon permeate the novelty records of all black vocal groups including, of course, The Coasters.

Rhythm and blues was something of an experiment for major labels and The Robins were not impressed with their treatment: 'RCA was just getting into the r & b field and the guy that was in charge didn't know anything about it,' complained Terrell, 'I used to be so disgusted going to their studios 'cos it was like a hole in the wall. I was under the impression that at RCA you would have the equivalent of Mantovani but the Shorty Rogers band wasn't as big as the Johnny Otis group. There were big acts on RCA—The Four Escorts, Gary Crosby—and we wanted that treatment, maybe even violins. But when we got inside, there was Shorty Rogers with all the head gear on—the great Shorty Rogers was directing this three piece group.'[17] If the 'popular' label manager at RCA had little experience of marketing r & b, the prestige which accompanied a major label contract was undeniably good for the group, Bobby Nunn: 'Until then we'd done shows for mixed audiences at joints with a rope down the middle and when everybody got high, they'd take the rope up themselves. The RCA records didn't click but they were played like mad and they got us on a lot of shows in L.A. We played The Oasis, The Hollywood Bowl, and The Waldorf Cellar and we were really immaculate, stone professional with white suits, bow-ties white shoes, hats, and canes. Everybody wore their process right like Sugar Ray Robinson—Billy Ward and the Dominoes commanded respect but their act wasn't as choreographed as ours and The Ravens heard us at The Oasis and Jimmy Ricks came up and told me, "You're the only group that I was really worried about." '[18]

When the RCA contract expired in December 1953, a quick session at Modern—without Leiber and Stoller—provided four cuts on the subsidiary label, Crown. While their familiarity makes for easy enjoyment, all were derivative. Chapman—who, between stints as The Robins' lead singer, did indeed spend periods in prison—was now consumed with a passion for Clyde McPhatter and sung, 'Double Crossin' Baby', a fairly obvious pinch of 'Have Mercy Baby' (Federal 12068) which Clyde had taken up to the top of the r & b charts with The Dominoes in 1952. 'I made a Vow', a Nunn–Chapman duet, was a doo-wop ballad—perfectly nice if thoroughly indistinguishable from literally thousands of others in the competitive, close harmony style—while 'Key to my Heart', a storming jump blues, resembled many a Clovers record. 'All I do is Rock' was redolent of Ivory Joe Hunter's 1950 smash, 'I almost lost my mind' (MGM 10578). Fortunately, The Robins' next recordings—with Leiber and Stoller—were thoroughly unrivalled in terms of originality and inventiveness.

Late in 1953, Leiber and Stoller decided to start their own record company and publishing company. They had observed how companies mistreated their performers by buying them the occasional expensive car instead of paying regular royalties and they realized that, young and inexperienced, they could expect to be similarly exploited.

With a record company and a publishing company of their own, they could be sure of collecting all the royalties that would be due to them. 'At the time,' said Bobby Nunn, 'they were kids just out of school. They were living right there in the coloured district down on Pico. Man, these guys knew what they were doing. I heard 'em say "We're gonna be millionaires in a couple of years." '[19]

CHAPTER TWO

# 'WE WEREN'T THE WORLD'S GREATEST PRODUCERS, WE WERE JUST STARTING'

DATELINE Hollywood 27 February 1954. 'Spark records, headed by A. L. Stoller, bowed recently with two releases in the rhythm and blues market. Label has set Gil Bernal, veteran tenor-man, and Willie and Ruth on their first sides. Lester Sill has been named national sales manager, with Jack Levy repping the firm in the East. Song scribes Jerry Leiber and Mike Stoller, who penned the click "Hound Dog" of last year, will handle a & r work for the firm.'

*Billboard* announced the formation of Spark records on 6 March 1954; more recently Mike Stoller described the situation in greater detail: 'My Dad and a friend of Lester Sill put up about 3,500 dollars each and we started a record company, a publishing company (Quintet Music) and a distributing company. We had an office and it was like a store, you could practically touch both walls with your arms outstretched. It was on Crenshaw Boulevard in Los Angeles. There was a glass front window with no curtains so you could see all the activity from the street. You opened up and there was an old oak desk, the kind that are used in the grammar schools, and behind that was a sofa facing the opposite way and a few steps from that was the piano facing in again and behind that—separated by a thin wood partition—was a filing cabinet and behind that was the back door which you could walk out of to get to the toilet. We used to have our rehearsals there, standing on top of the sofa and on top of the desk. We made our records at a studio run by a man called Abe Robyn, he was called Bunny because he looked like a rabbit. He wasn't called Bunny because his name was Bernard or anything, it was Abe, but he looked like a rabbit and he would suck his teeth sometimes and he would look even more like a rabbit. But he was a terrific technician and he had two machines at a studio called Masters Recorders on Fairfax Avenue a couple of miles from our office. We would occasionally over dub; everything was cut mono and if we wanted to add something we would go from one mono track, transferring everything including the live signal, on to the new one and balance as we went and that was the only way we could do it. We only assigned the matrix numbers when we released the record, I think. We didn't ever call out on the tape *this is LS 13* or *LS 14*. That's something that's insisted upon by outfits like CBS or RCA. We would say, *"Riot in Cell Block No. 9" take one, take two,* and so on. As we cut the master I think that's probably when we assigned a matrix number.'

Stoller himself played piano on virtually all the Spark recordings but, for other instruments, he and Leiber hired the cream of Los Angeles rhythm and blues musicians. 'We used Charlie Norris, a blues guitarist, for most of the stuff and Barney Kessel on one or two sides. The upright bass player was Ralph Hamilton and it was probably Jesse Sailes on drums. Gil Bernal, who played tenor saxophone on "Riot", "I love Paris", and "Loop de Loop Mambo", was a Mexican–American. I hired Gil because I went to school with him at City College. We were taking a music class together and that's how I met him, he and I used to hang out across the street from the college.'

Over a period of eighteen months, Spark issued over twenty-two records including sides by The Honeybears, black balladeer Ernie Andrews, several blues by Ray Agee. Big Boy Groves, and Mister Ruffin and 'Love Me' by Willie and Ruth whose original version—the worst song they ever wrote, according to Leiber and Stoller—was revived by Elvis Presley on a million-selling EP record (RCA–Victor EPA 992) in 1956. 'The Honeybears,' said Stoller, 'were a gospel group from San Francisco who we persuaded to sing secular music. Then we had another group on the label who were made up of the lead singer of The Honeybears and this gal singer and it was called Willie and Ruth. His name was Wiley but we called him Willie; Ruth was either a wife or a girl-friend or a sister of one of the other people in the group. We'd gone to hear them sing in San Francisco after seeing a distributor there.'

But Leiber and Stoller were not entirely preoccupied with their own label. Linda Hopkins was brought in from San Francisco to make a number of recordings which were sold to Crystalette and 'Black Denim Trousers', one of a number of songs for a trio called Gil, Bert and Sally, came out on Capitol (3219) as by The Cheers. A top twenty smash in December 1955, it was Leiber and Stoller's first national hit. Like 'Love Me' it cannot, however, be one of which they are proud and listening to it now one is reminded of Tin Pan Alley's inept reactions to the success of genuine rock 'n' roll.

Of all Leiber and Stoller's many activities during this period none was more important than their work for Spark with The Robins who undoubtedly became the label's main attraction. From a total of twelve recordings made at three separate sessions, they issued six singles, some of which sold very well in and around Los Angeles.

'We didn't,' said Stoller, 'have any really good distribution except we were very fortunate in Los Angeles, I guess partially because the group was local and was appearing there regularly. Some of those records sold as many as eighty or ninety thousand copies in Los Angeles; we'd sell a few thousand in San Francisco, six records in Ohio somewhere and that would be it. Our partner, Lester Sill, he would generally deal with the promotion. I can remember on a few occasions running with the record in my hand to the disc-jockey, Hunter Hancock. He was a white disc-jockey who played only black records. He had his little studio and had a kind of obnoxious patter that he kept going all the time, and I can remember running up to his place with the record in my grubby fist—a 78 yet.'

The roots of many popular black quartets of the period lay in the histrionically impassioned, ecstatically abandoned harmonies of gospel groups like The Five Blind Boys of Mississippi or The Sensational Nightingales. With one or two alterations the love of a girl could be expressed with the same fervour as a love of God. Other groups, particularly after the success of The Penguins 'Earth Angel' (Dootone 348) in 1954, absorbed an idealistic white concept of love and, in this context, their lyrics were invariably sentimental and often pathetic. In the hands of Leiber and Stoller, The Robins continued to eschew both sentimental and gospel-influenced styles in favour of traditional blues attitudes. Whatever the style, the best post-war rhythm and blues is characterized by an orientation towards black adults rather than black or, indeed, white children. Once upon a time records were said to have 'soul' when they expressed deeply felt, mature problems and, by these standards the records of The Robins were exceptionally good r & b, striking deep into the heart of ghetto life. Later pop records by The Coasters were wholly concerned with frustrations of an entirely juvenile character; to some extent they had to absorb the values of White America. There was never any question of The Robins attempting to do either. The characters of their songs shirked their responsibilities, got drunk, went to jail, treated sex in naturally easy and good-humoured terms and encountered prejudice each day of their lazy, promiscuous lives.

On one of The Robins most important records—'Riot in Cell Block No. 9'—the lead is taken by Richard Berry, an influential if sorely underestimated figure who never appeared on stage as a member of the group. He was born in New Orleans in 1935 but, like other important black West Coast singers, had moved from the Deep South to seek employment in California during or shortly after World War II. Arriving in Los Angeles, he played piano for a succession of local groups and began writing songs with Jesse Belvin, father figure to a great many younger singers. With

Jesse's assistance, Berry became the archetypal session vocalist, a position he retained until the early sixties when tastes shifted away from traditional vocal groups towards commercial soul.

He first sang with The Flairs, an influential group from whom The Coasters obtained two of their personnel during the mid-fifties. The quintet—Cornelius Gunter, Thomas Fox, Obediah 'Young' Jessie, Beverley Thompson, and Berry—recorded for Flair, a subsidiary of Modern, where, as Berry recalls, they also worked with Leiber and Stoller: 'You know what is surprising about those cats? Before almost anybody knew anything about them they did "She wants to Rock" (Flair 1012), the first record I made with The Flairs in 1953. Joe Bihari took us over and introduced us and Mike and Jerry had all that shit, bang, bang, that shooting and shit. They were the ones who put that in there. That's where their heads were then.'[1] 'She wants to Rock' is a pounding choral groover on which Berry sings lead and the rest of the group (in parentheses) chant lines in an arrangement which Leiber and Stoller were soon to perfect with The Robins and The Coasters:

*'Well I come in from work, tired and sore*
*she meets me rockin' at the door*
*I said "Ease up baby can't you see*
*real good rockin' be the death of me"* (*She wants to rock*)
*I tried to hop* (*she wouldn't stop*)
*I called the cops* (*she grabbed a gun*)
*I started to run* (*she said "don't go"*)
*I hit the door* (*gunshots*) *bang! bang! bang!*
*Aaaaow help me somebody 'fore she rocks me through the floor.'*

'After they had got the Robins,' continued Berry, 'Leiber and Stoller called me to do that "Riot in Cell Block No. 9". They told me just how they wanted me to do it and everything.'[2] The Robins usual bass singer, Bobby Nunn, had a comparatively soft burr to his voice. It betrayed a friendly disposition and Leiber and Stoller were after a real psychopath: 'We always went for the sound that we thought would be the best for a given song,' explained Stoller. 'We borrowed voices from people who weren't regular members of the group on occasion and there were various lead singers including Richard Berry on "Riot in Cell Block No. 9", Bobby Nunn on "Framed", and Grady Chapman on "I Love Paris". The Richards brothers and Ty Terrell didn't sing lead at all. They usually sang "doo-wah, doo-wah" and had their hands up in the air like that,' Stoller waves his fingers. 'We tried Bobby Nunn on "Riot" but he didn't seem to get the right quality, it just didn't happen right so we got hold of Richard Berry.'

Berry fulfilled all their requirements with a very convincing characterization. A siren wails; gunfire spurts; tenor and drummer snap out BOM bom BOM bom BOM and in comes Berry, languid, cool, menacing, and as nasty as a guy doing time for armed robbery should be.

*'On July the second 1953*
*I was servin' time for armed robbery*
*At 4 o'clock in the morning I was sleeping in my cell*
*I heard a whistle blow—then I heard somebody yell*

*There's a riot goin' on* x 3
*up in cell block number nine*

*The trouble started in cell block number fo'*
*spread like fire across the prison floor*
*I said, "Okay boys get ready to run*
*here comes the warden with a tommy-gun".*

*There's a . . .*

*The warden said, "Come out with your hands up in the air—*
*if you don't stop this riot you all gonna get the chair"*
*Scarface Jones said, "It's too late to quit—*
*pass the dynamite 'cos the fuse is lit."'*

The electric chair poses no threat and wardens with submachine guns are no deterrent. Every now and then there's a riot goin' on and when it is you know that Berry wants to be right there handing round the dynamite. One especially gruff member of the chorus appears to be suffering from a severe attack of laryngitis. His throatiness and Gil Bernal's tenor saxophone, wailing high and loud between verses, helps to increase a tense and violent atmosphere.

Since Richard Berry was contracted to Modern records at the time, all concerned—including Atlantic's public relations department—have long encouraged the false impression that Bobby Nunn was responsible for Richard's incredible narration. The Robins sold 90,000 copies largely on the strength of it but that didn't help Richard's career or his bank balance. He crossed over Melrose Avenue into Modern where he recorded his own version of the theme under the title of 'The Big Break' (Flair 1055).

*'Sittin' in my cell lookin' through the bars*
*at all the con men in the prison yard*
*it won't be long til' me an' my friend, Snake*
*get ready to make our—prison break.*

*Now run, run real fast.*

*At twelve o'clock sharp the guard comes by*
*that's when I let out my crazy cry*
*Ma stomach hurts, man, ah'm sick*
*He opens the door—Snake let's flit*

*Now run . . .*

*The warder told me when I first got in*
*"if you be cool daddy we can all be friends"*
*but I started riots an' now I'm in for life*
*so without further hesitations I will make my flight.'*

'I wrote "The Big Break",' said Berry, 'That was a spin-off

from "Riot in Cell Block No. 9". See when the Bihari brothers found out that I was the lead singer on that, they wanted me to come back and cover it with something else. Like most of the things I did with The Flairs, it sold well but I had to sue 'em for back royalties. I think I got about 1,800 dollars out of a 50,000 dollar suit and it took me five years to get that. You're talking about the days of exploiters and slave-traders!"[3]

'The Big Break' was issued on 16 October 1954 and round about that time, The Robins cut 'Framed' with Bobby Nunn who imitates every nuance of Richard Berry's narrative style:

*'I was walkin' down the street minding my own affairs*
*when two policemen grabbed me—er unawares*
*they said, "Is your name Henry?" I said, "Why sure"*
*they say "You the boy we bin lookin' for".*

*Framed, I was framed*
*I never do nothin' wrong*
*but I always get blamed, framed.*

*They put me in the line-up an' let the bright light shine*
*there were ten po' souls like me standin' in that line*
*ah knew I was the victim of someone's evil plan*
*when a stool pigeon walked in an' said, "Er—That's the Man."*

*Framed ...*

*The prosecutin' attorney started prosecutin' me*
*man, that cat gave me the third degree*
*he said, "Where were you the night of er June twenty-nine?"*
*I said, "I was home in bed" he said, 'Jury this man is lyin' "*

*Framed ...*

*I denied the charges of robbin' the liquor store*
*denied the charges of carryin' a forty-fo'*
*denied the charges of vagrancy too*
*but when the judge came down poured whisky on my head*
*turned around to the jury an' said,*
*"convict this man he is drunk!"*
*what could I do?'*

'Framed', perhaps the most ingenious of all Leiber and Stoller's compositions, is likely to have been the prototype for a great many records which referred to legal proceedings in terms which the black audience found particularly relevant. But the voices on 'Divorce Court' (The Five Dutones, One-derful 4815) or the numerous versions of 'Here comes The Judge' were rarely as effective as the narrator of 'Framed' whose resignation to the events he unfolds is expressed in a half-dead pan, half-vacillatory speech conveying an air of oppression and bewilderment as well as the humour with which unpleasant situations are occasionally remembered. Both 'Riot in Cell Block No. 9' and 'Framed' were copied in 1954 (the former inspired covers by Wanda Jackson, and Vicki Young with Big Dave's orchestra) but their influence continued to grow throughout the sixties when, not only blacks, but all other minority groups were increasingly inclined to politicize their status. By the early seventies, in the aftermath of the Folsom strike, Attica and Kent State, The Beach Boys and Sly and The Family Stone —significantly both California based—made variants which used the same dramatic tune or philosophy to convey equally controversial if, in many respects, surprisingly less inflammatory messages.

Seemingly unaffected by such revolutionary struggles, founder member of The Coasters, Billy Guy, made a somewhat soft-centred version of 'The Big Break' (as 'The Prison Break') for Lloyd Price's Double L label in the mid-sixties. Unissued in the USA it was made available in Britain on an album entitled 'Hungry' (Joy 189) in 1971. Invariably a comedian, Guy adds a 'Down the hall, over the wall' refrain and a final verse which is missing from the original. Having surmounted the final obstacle to freedom, he's faced by a monster: eight feet tall, covered in slime and with eyes that light up the night. He flees back to safe custody: 'Lord, I'm so happy to be back in my cell,' he chortles. Richard Berry would not have approved.

Berry's conflict with the judiciary continued beyond his guest-artist relationship with The Robins. If rhythm and blues is the vehicle for personal expression that is commonly supposed, Berry must have cut most of his early sides while on parole. 'Next Time' (Flair 1071), made in 1955, prolongs this dialogue in a witty and predictable fashion: after catching his baby entertaining another man he leaves his pad to be faced with rent arrears which he tried to avoid:

'*Well after the confusion had all died down*
*I figure I'd better get out of town*
*but when I arrived at the airport*
*there stood a man with a note "failure to support"*

*Next time, next time I say's no next time baby*
*that was last time.*

*Well they took me to see that friend of mine*
*Yeah district court, room two-twenty nine*
*The judge said "your payments are way behind"*
*I said, "don't worry daddy, it won't happen next time."*'

Like his other 'judicial' songs, gutty blues riffs punctuate his narration which, on this occasion, bears some melodic similarity to 'I don't know' which the blues singer, Willie Mabon, had written and recorded in Chicago two years before (Parrot 1050).

The nature of Berry's other narrations, 'Riot', and 'The Big Break', are reminiscent of Sgt. Joe Friday, hero of the then popular television crime serial 'Dragnet', whose similarly dead-pan, 'Jus' the facts Ma'am' delivery punctuated a menacing staccato orchestration at the beginning of the programme. Joe Friday cropped up again in 1957—as one of many fictional sleuths to which The Coasters referred in 'Searchin''.

If legal proceedings were Berry's main preoccupation during this period, women were a close rival for his attentions. In addition to his many sides with the original Flairs, other records for Flair and RPM from 1953 to 1956 were very largely slow and ethereal tales of romantic love. 'Please Tell Me' (Flair 1064), 'Wait for Me' (RPM 477), and 'Together' (Flair 1075) would recall the craftsmanship of the Moonglows had Berry not been accompanied by an excruciatingly dull female group. Credited as The Dreamers, they were capable of a more lively back-up when the tempo increased. 'Daddy Daddy' (Flair 1058) and 'Good Love' (RPM 477) are both fine jump items with musicianly piano and saxophone breaks from Ike Turner's orchestra. 'Yama Yama Pretty Mama' (RPM 465), recorded in New Orleans with pianist Jimmy Beasley, is something else again; a quite astonishing Little Richard imitation.

Berry also became 'Henry' for 'Roll with me Henry'—recorded by Etta James as 'Wallflower' (Modern 947)—where he answered Miss James' direct sexual invitation with a casual eagerness. He is heard to wail compliance in the chorus on the other side of the record, 'Hold me, squeeze me', and his grief-stricken sobs are also to the fore on Donald Woods 'Death of an Angel' (Flip 306). His final single for Flair was 'Jelly Roll' (1075), a not uncommon ode in praise of the female pudendum.

Late in 1956, Berry went to Max Freitag's Flip label where, with a new group, The Pharaohs, he came close to a national hit with his second release, 'Louie, Louie' (321). Here again it's an entirely different Richard Berry with a quaint West Indian accent to his baritone voice and a calypso feel to his phrasing. It sold well in the r & b market but national honours went six years later to the musically incompetent white group, The Kingsmen. It was the kind of justice which Berry had gotten used to. Some of the Flip material seems to have been deliberately slanted towards the white pop lists—'No kissin' and a Huggin'' (318) bears more than a strong resemblance to Paul Anka's 'Tell me that you love me'—but in the main he remained faithful to black oral traditions. Frank Zappa has recalled being attuned to the delights of acappella singing by Berry who told Frank how the Pharaohs got together in the dark in order to perfect their harmonies. And some of these are very delicate indeed. The moods are fragile as if harmony was a collection of gossamer strands to be scattered by a draught under the studio door. 'Have Love will Travel' (349) is a complex up-tempo side with a workmanlike bass and a nice touch in train imitations while 'Take The Key' (318), where Richard sings in a pure and gentle falsetto, is especially appealing.

Berry left Flip in 1958 and, since then, it has been downhill all the way. Staying in Los Angeles he cut once-off records for a string of small independent labels—Paxley, Hasil, K & G—which Kim Fowley and Gary Paxton either owned or produced. I've not heard them all but Paxton is invariably the hallmark of a worse than useless record and, a report to the effect that they were made at S and L Recorders in El Monte where the engineer, Harold Shock, was in his seventies and deaf in one ear, is not altogether promising. A couple on Smash in 1963 included Berry's impression of Arthur Prysock on Harlan Howard's country ballad, 'Empty Chair' (Smash 1811); there is really no end to the man's versatility but good fortune has persistently eluded him. Billy Guy has recently compared Berry's ill-luck with that of the neglected Jesse Belvin:

'Yes, it was Richard Berry on "Riot in Cell Block No. 9". He was a master. We used him because one of the guys couldn't do what Leiber and Stoller wanted him to do. That's one of the best writers on the coast man that really got ripped off. Richard Berry wrote many a tune that you've heard that's got all kinds of names on it. Him and Jesse Belvin had it sewed up. They'd sell their songs or people would steal them.'

Berry did however manage to ensure that he was credited with writing a number of exceptionally fine r & b records including, 'Chains' by Little Esther Phillips (Warwick 559), 'Good Rockin' Daddy' (Modern 962), another success for Etta James; 'Moments' (Amazon 1003), a top fifty hit in 1962 for the black songstress, Jennell Hawkins and, of course, many of his own recordings, 'Louie Louie' included. 'Go Go Girl' (AMC 818) by Richard Berry and the Soul-Searchers was a half-hearted attempt to be fashionable in 1965 but since then Berry hasn't been heard, except by patrons of clubs in West LA who go to dance to his versions of recent Motown hits.

While 'Framed' and 'Riot in Cell Block No. 9' are both historic recordings in the development of groupdom, The Robins made ten other sides for Spark; some, it is true, display less originality but still have a great deal to commend them. 'The Hatchet Man', from their first session, is a particularly witty sexual metaphor; to a chorus of 'be oodlee bop-chop chop' the lead singer wields his axe all the way from Maine to Tennessee. Along the way he compares his progress—and potency—to that of 'Lovin' Dan', the hero of 'Sixty Minute Man' by The Dominoes (Federal 12022), the best-selling r & b record of 1951.

*'Looka here girls I'm tellin' you now*
*they call me lovin' Dan*
*I rock 'em, roll 'em all night long*
*I'm a Sixty Minute Man.'*

'There were often references from one record to another,' said Stoller. 'Not what they call an answer record which was a direct copy, a direct response. But there were often cross references to characters that emerged in one song and this dialogue was carried on through records like "Hatchet Man".'

Bill Brown, lead on The Dominoes record, had a rich bass profundo derived, perhaps from the Harmonizing Four and other long-established gospel groups. The voice of 'The Hatchet Man', alias Bobby Nunn, is a world-weary monotone firmly rooted in the blues. While 'Lovin' Dan' may be a passionate lover, 'The Hatchet Man' has an equally considerable technique:

*'Now if you got sixty minutes call up Lovin' Dan*
*but if you want sumpin' choppin' call the hatchet man.'*

or

*'Now Lovin' Dan may knock you out*
*but the hatchet man will make you jump an' shout.'*

Like the chorus of 'Sixty Minute Man', that in 'The Hatchet Man' contains some similar specifics. 'Lovin' Dan' could only aspire to sixty minutes; Nunn's hatchet will chop you down like a cherry tree if it takes all night.

Using blatant phrases which are often reminiscent of Hank Ballard's 'Annie' songs 'Wrap it Up' treats sex less ambiguously. In 'Work with me, Annie' (Federal 12169) Ballard had pleaded, 'Annie please don't cheat/give me all my meat' and The Robins offer some similarly lecherous advice:

*'Mmmm you look so sweet* (*Wrap it up*)
*mmm you're a treat* (*Wrap it up*)
*well can't be beat* (*Wrap it up*)
*mmm got cute little feet* (*Wrap it up*)
*oh you my meat* (*Wrap it up*)
*well, wrap it up baby an' save it all for me.'*

Melodically, the final instruction corresponds to Ballard's 'Work with me Annie—let's git it while the gittin' is good'. 'The Hatchet Man', in particular, exploits, in humorous fashion, the common myth relating to the black man's extraordinary genital development. This, and many more post-war r & b songs—Bullmoose Jackson's 'Big Ten Inch Record' (King 4580), The Swallows' 'It ain't the Meat' (King 4501), and others—maintained the use of sexual symbolism which had been far more frequent in blues recordings before the war. 'Wrap it Up', a duet with Bobby Nunn, introduces the smoky and distinctive voice of Carl Gardner who has explained, at length, why The Robins are blues rather than gospel-orientated:

'I myself went to church with my mother and father when I was a kid. I had plenty of uncles an' aunts who were teachers, an' er some were doctors, an' I saw in church that they'd be sitting up the front. I was a very young kid, and—oh I was about thirteen years old—an' I would sit at the back of the church with my mother an' father. We were a very poor family, they raised five of us. I would notice that all the people who had money were sittin' in the very front pews an' I would say this church—this church business is not correct. I was thinkin' I'm gonna quit goin' to church because I don't believe that God would let all the rich folks sit up there; I says I'm as good as those people sittin' up front. I'm thinkin' I'm gonna quit church an' find my own thing. So when I started singin' I was learnin' somethin'. I didn't only just go on the road to travel just to sing. I was studying myself, y'know. Finding me. I went through all phases including Islam with Malcolm X. I studied everythin' an' didn't come to any conclusion as to what I wanted to be, but my beliefs are in Islam more so than in Christianity which, at that time—Christianity in Texas was jus' y'know—everybody was jivin' man—they were—this is church but everybody was, y'know all the rich were there. So the moral of my story is I didn't get any good Christian tunes under my belt. I used to sing in church when I was very young but they were straight such as 'The Old Rugged

Cross', an' like er—no Aretha Franklin feelings—so the blues was always somethin' I preferred. I love the blues. Roy Brown was a great favourite of mine. Charles Brown was another an' we had small bands then like er Mr. Cleanhead Vinson. Eddie Cleanhead an' Ray Charles came along at that time—he influenced me. An later people like er—he's from Mississippi—only plays guitar an' sings deep down South blues er—Muddy, he influenced me. S'funny thing I was interested in—not screamin', not gospel blues like the James Brown thing. I never liked anybody screamin' y'know. I liked the deep feelings in blues an' the troubles that people have from the blues—y'see the black man was singin' the blues becos' he was down an' er he had no freedom in America. He had no—nothin' to do but make up words an' sing lyrics of—about himself. So blues is sorta folk-lore black to me—that kind of blues it was like "Hey man, I'm so depressed, y'know I'm so down that—that I wanna let this out an' tell the people how I feel. Most of the tunes that we bin cutting are not as bluesy as they should be—in fact, the're semi-blues that we were doin'.'

Late-comer to The Robins, but a founder member of The Coasters, Carl Gardner was born in Tyler, Texas in 1928 where, gospel excepted, he heard and enjoyed a rich and surprisingly eclectic variety of musical styles. Carol, one of his two sisters, preferred opera and now makes a living as an operatic singer in New York. While Carl found blues more to his liking, the popular hits of Hoagy Carmichael, Nat King Cole, and Billy Eckstine had an indelible impact. The now-declining Texan big bands, including Milt Larkins band in which Eddie 'Cleanhead' Vinson sang, featured not only blues based arrangements but a heavy sprinkling of current hits; 'Old Buttermilk Sky', 'I'm in the Mood for Love', 'The Very Thought of You', and others which, with a little imagination, became an easy vehicle for a personal blues interpretation. Carl Gardner has remained a repressed dance-band vocalist to this day:

'The guy I used to sing with had an all school-teacher

band, everybody could read well an' everythin'. I was playin' drums then, best to my ability, er I was singin' the blues an' playin' the drums at the same time. Another guy we used would sometimes come along an' I'd get off the drums an' get up an' sing tunes like "Mona Lisa", "Stardust", an' er "Serenadin' the Blues"—tunes like that. It was LaSalle Gunther's band. We had eight or nine pieces an' we played all over Texas mostly for the real elite. Where I came from there was millionaires in my home town, mostly rich, white oil-well people. I was only about sixteen or seventeen then —playin' drums and singin'—but I must have been picking up like—oh thirty, maybe forty dollars a night. An' I was good at it. I do the blues very well but y'know I sing pop much better becos' I er—the pop field has always interested me such as "Stardust" an' things like that.'

Lasalle Gunther's band worked in and around Tyler at night while Carl worked in a department store during the day. A German classical pianist who had trained his sister, taught Carl the rudiments of musical theory and gave him a hundred popular songs to learn by heart. By 1951 he was sufficiently professional to move to the West Coast and approach name bands. Arriving in Los Angeles, Carl hung around the 5–4 Ballroom on 54th and Broadway and smaller clubs on Western Avenue, continually asking each and every band if he could do a number with them. Putting his face around had initially good results when the combo of jazz pianist and Dootone recording artist, Carl Perkins, backed him on several gigs at which Gardner sang 'Autumn Leaves', 'Serenadin' the Blues', and other standard fare. His career changed direction entirely when Johnny Otis introduced him to The Robins during a gig at The Oasis.

'There I met the Robins an' their manager, Lester Sill, who was also Leiber and Stoller's manager. Y'know I was out there—I had just come from Texas tryin' to get in the business as a single. I was lookin' for some big band, tryin' to get with Duke Ellington or Count Basie. The big band was hangin', it was just level, it was nice y'know. An' suddenly POW! Rhythm an' blues took over an' big bands fell down. After a couple of weeks with The Robins, Lester says, "either you sing these particular tunes, Carl, or we just have to forget it". I says, "O.K. money's first" so I took this group thing. I wanted to do pop tho'.' Carl joined Roy and Billy Richards, Ty Terrell, and Bobby Nunn in The Robins when their lead singer, Grady Chapman, went 'into some kind of home er—institution or somethin'. They needed a lead singer an' they got me so I started doin' Grady's stuff which was "Ten Days in Jail" an' a few others on stage while he was put away. They were supposed to let me go but they decided to keep me even when Grady got out an' started doin' harmonizin' an' some lead also. So there was about eight Robins man.' Said Bobby Nunn, 'Carl came in 'cos Grady had problems. We had a concert with Earl Bostic in 1954 but Grady was in jail so Carl deputized. He really blew the concert but we kept him on 'cos he had heart.'[4]

Gardner sings lead on seven of The Robins recordings for Spark, including the only ballads made for the label. The lyrically sad themes associated with the blues dominate both. Neither 'Just like a Fool' nor 'If Teardrops were Kisses' are typical doo-wop ballads as Jean Charles Marion, when reviewing the latter, has carefully noted: 'On this The Robins offer a ballad that features a great vocal ascending ladder—from bass to high tenor—at transitional breaks in the arrangement. The melody line is a pretty one, accented by a strong lead vocal delivery.'[5] And indeed the interlocking bass and high tenor behind Gardner effectively create an air of desperation. Moreover, thematically, both this and 'Just like a Fool' are a long way removed from the frequent boy meets girl situation where a preoccupation with first love is more often seen in a wholly unreal, immature and magical light. Gardner's vocal is particularly expressive; he is fully aware that love is not necessarily eternal as he sings:

*'If my sorrows were joy life would be an easy game'* or *'soon you'll see a change in me,*
*the chains of love are broken and now I'm free.'*

Clearly, human relationships change and love can bring attendant frustrations.

Very rarely, when they were not trying or, perhaps trying too hard, Leiber and Stoller could be as robotic as any of today's bubble-gum song-writers. 'Loop de Loop Mambo' has no mordant wit and one or two passages ('you look so fantastic when you mambo, you're just like elastic when you mambo') succeed in making the listener wince. But, with its references to Puerto Rico and Havana, it was the first of Leiber and Stoller's compositions to emphasize a rhythm of which they were particularly fond: 'Boogie', as the song says, but 'with a Latin beat'. *Billboard* liked it—'the group really rides this one with a spectacular treatment of a solid piece of material. The lads get in on the current dance craze with an item that has a freshness, drive, and novelty'—and Gil Bernal takes one of his finest solos.

From the outset, with Floyd Dixon and Little Willie Littlefield in 1951 and 1952, the songs of Leiber and Stoller have included space for a solo, sometimes piano but more often a saxophone, between the second and third verse. Bernal, who also cut his own sides for Spark—'The Whip' (102) and 'Strawberry Stomp' (106)—occupies this slot on eight of The Robins tracks. Often confused with King Curtis, whom he resembles on 'Wrap it Up', Bernal displays less of the fancy, if appropriate, embellishments for which Curtis became the most widely acclaimed of all rock 'n' roll tenor-players. Bernal was not always in total command of his instrument and in an attempt to be light and frothy on 'If Teardrops were Kisses', he winds up his break with three discordant notes in succession. But compared to King Curtis, he was plainer, muddier, and altogether dirtier where it counts, particularly on up-tempo numbers. He is suitably crazy on 'Loop de Loop Mambo'—where he plays an unusual reed full of spittle effect—and 'I Love Paris', a mangled version of the standard by acid-voiced Grady Chapman, is chiefly interesting for Bernal's extended solo where, like Paris in the summer, he really sizzles.

Leiber and Stoller rarely worked with women singers or, for that matter, men with a conventional high tenor lead like Grady Chapman. He sings out front on one other Spark cut and, like 'I Love Paris', rhythmically and vocally, 'Whadaya Want', is undistinguished. The lyrics were, nonetheless, of considerable interest.

'I was and still am, I guess, primarily interested in a kind of social satire and a great source of material has always been the situation of the poor, the joke that the poor tell on themselves,'[6] recalled Jerry Leiber. Thematically, 'Whadaya Want' offers an early and unusual slant on this conception. Southern Californians belong to the richest society the world has ever known. A world where the acquisitive urge knows no bounds, where materialistic values afflict the entire white population, including today's affluent hippies. Racial minority groups have long been excluded by design if not choice and The Robins occupied another world altogether. In 'Whadaya Want', Chapman expresses a sane denial of social status. He prefers a little girl's love to a flashy car/caviar/aeroplane/house in Spain/pink champagne/motorboat/cashmere coat or, by implication, any of the other symbols of nearby Beverley Hills, Brentwood, and Bel Air. Marie Adams explored a similar theme with the Johnny Otis Show on 'All I Want is Your Love' (Capitol 14837—issued only in England). Jerry Leiber also returned to it in the Coasters 'What about Us' in 1959, but the highly stylized performance on that and other Coasters records began to evolve with their final recordings with The Robins. It is all too easy to assume that the need to prevent imitations was one of the simpler reasons behind this development.

The practice of duplicating the entire sound of a particular performance with another artist and succeeding with the 'cover' version on the strength of advanced distribution was not wholly confined to the white record industry. The King label in Cincinnati made a small fortune from doing so largely from the activities of black a & r man Henry Glover who covered Joe Liggin's 'Honeydripper' (Specialty 338), with Bullmoose Jackson (King 4100), and a host of West Coast hits, including some by Richard Berry and the Hollywood Flames, with Little Willie John. Glover explained his modus operandi in 'Blues Unlimited': 'I had just heard about a record that had come out of California that was a hit. I had the record in Cincinnatti so fast no one ever heard of the (original) group. We got the record out on the street before they ever got it distributed.' He was referring to a cover by The Charms of The Jewels, 'Hearts of Stone' (R & B 1301), but, doubtless, similar methods enabled the same group to cover 'Whadaya Want' (Deluxe 6080). Without any sophisticated means of distribution, Leiber and Stoller suffered with 'Riot in Cell Block No. 9' at the hands of Capitol and now Henry Glover had demonstrated the ease with which he had been able to profit from the ideas of their own writing and production. But while Leiber and Stoller's records became increasingly difficult to duplicate, cover records did not annoy them. Mike Stoller: 'In fact, I was always delighted to have people do cover versions. I'm a songwriter, Jerry felt the same way. I didn't think Vicki Young's record was good. I thought it was ludicrous just as, at that time, I thought that many of Capitol's attempts to imitate our records or even take our songs without our production would come out ludicrous and they did. Capitol, Decca—those West Coast companies that we knew, unless we produced them—I'm not saying we were the world's greatest producers, we were just starting—but they had no concept and they would take these songs—we knew how they were supposed to go—and they would do them in a very old-fashioned way. If the records we made began to get more complicated, it wasn't to avoid cover records, it was just the way we were moving.'

'I Must be Dreaming'—where an invitation to dance is received with a promise of more exciting things to follow—rolls along in an unselfconscious and seemingly uncontrived fashion:

*'Well I met her in a dance-hall—in Tennessee,*
*I smiled at her she smiled at me*
*I said "baby it would move me*
*if I could dance with you"*
*she said, "anything that moves you daddy s'gonna move me too".'*

But it was the last occasion on which the records of The Robins or, subsequently The Coasters, contained any such spontaneous ingredients. Their very next record—'Smokey Joe's Cafe'—displayed many of the carefully contrived and exceedingly well integrated lyrical and musical qualities for which The Coasters were to become internationally famous.

A tenth of California's twenty million inhabitants are Mexican–Americans. A large proportion live in Los Angeles where the Chicano rock 'n' roll singer, Ritchie Valens, enjoyed his most devoted following. West Texas and California, in particular, offer a paradise to the many wretchedly poor Mexican families across the Rio Grande.

Lured by the promise of employment and better conditions, they migrate, in thousands, to Tucson, San Diego, and Los Angeles where they have long competed with blacks for the lower-paid jobs in factories, kitchens, and food-processing plants. From 'Down in Mexico' in 1957 to 'Teach me how to Shimmy'—where Billy Guy could hully-gully as well as 'Chico'—in 1961, the compositions of Leiber and Stoller, not infrequently contain Mexican references. 'Smokey Joe's Cafe' was the first. Los Angeles has half as many Latin-American record companies as those devoted to r & b and the incorporation of Mexican elements was not necessarily Leiber and Stoller's attempt to appeal to a wider market. Nor did they intend to awaken the listener's sensibilities to the plight of the Chicano people who occupy a low—if not the lowest—stratum in American society. Cynics will say that their presence deserved mention for this reason alone but, in fact, Leiber and, particularly Stoller, had good reason to compose songs with Mexican elements: 'I was very interested, intrigued, and excited by Latin-American rhythms. One Easter vacation in New York I used to sit night after night and listen to Machito's band. This would be in the late 1940s—he was playing at the Clique Club which became Birdland. The use of similar rhythms in our songs, as well as the reference to Mexicans, was just an aspect of our lives at that time. I went to a high school when I first arrived in LA and it was ninety per cent Mexican–American. In fact I sometimes say that I was the only Jewish Pachuco. A Pachuco is a Mexican–American sub-culture that had its own styles of clothes, of cars, own style of dancing, own style of walking. Pachuco might mean what Chicano means today except that many Mexican–Americans rejected Pachuco culture; it was not Mexican culture but more of a ghetto culture in a way. It was separate, Pachucos didn't speak Spanish, they spoke Pachuco. They had Spanish words in it but different words for different things like cigarette was "frajco" and money was "jundo" and a parent was a "jefe" which mean't literally "chief".'

'Smokey Joe's Cafe' was one of the first in a long series of compact plays which dramatized aspects of a particularly seamy, sleazy, 'low-life' environment, situation or side of life. It belongs to the same category as the alleys, strip-clubs, pawnshops, street-corners, racetracks, blue light diners, and, of course, prisons which The Robins, and subsequently The Coasters, were required to sing about for over sixteen years. Lyrically, the clues are not obvious. You do not have to be of Mexican extraction to eat chili beans. Nevertheless, from the introductory vocal chant, a twice-repeated 'Waaah aah Smokey Joe's Cafe', the words are set to a heavy rhythm. It is precisely the sort of sound you would expect to hear in a bar-cum-beanery-cum-border-town brothel. 'Smokey Joe's Cafe' is undoubtedly a place in which to experience one's full share of strong sensations and dissonant kicks:

*'Ooh, one day while I was eatin' beans* (*at Smokey Joe's Cafe*)
*jus' sittin' diggin' all the scenes* (*at Smokey Joe's Cafe*)'.

While the heat is semi-tropical and the 'scenes' more than likely to increase the temperature, Carl Gardner is initially determined to preserve his cool. But like a number of Leiber and Stoller's characters, his self confidence is easily destroyed and the appearance of a red-hot senorita, drenched in sweet perfume, swaying with sinuous ease and dripping provocation, is enough to reduce him to a mass of nerve tissue:

*'she smiled at me my heart went boom*
*then everybody in the room* (*at Smokey Joe's Cafe*)
*they said, "Man be careful*
*that chick belongs to Smokey Joe."'*

Her advances unchecked, the assembled clientele utter an awed warning as one voice. Before Carl can recover, the jealous proprietor himself emerges and his use of cutlery is not confined to eating beans:

*'From behind the counter there came a man*
*a chef-hat on his head and a knife in his hands.'*

Who, apart from Chuck Berry, would have thought of the 'chef-hat'? It is this superficially simple yet deliciously neat kind of observation which places Jerry Leiber on a par with Chuck Berry as the foremost poets of rock 'n' roll. The singer could have made a run for it but he is ordered to swallow the very last morsel. It is easy to imagine Joe's satisfaction as Carl chokes over his plate:

*'He grabbed me by my collar an' began to shout*
*You better eat up all your beans an' boy then clear right on out.'*

In the final verse we are told that Carl would prefer to eat his chili beans at 'Jim's or Jack's or John's or Gene's', than to risk his life at the mercy of 'Smokey Joe' whose behaviour is consistent with that of the mass media stereotype Mexican cafe-owner; mean, stupid, greasy, hot-blooded, and quick-tempered. 'That Smokey Joe's a crazy fool.'

'Smokey Joe's Cafe' was the last record by The Robins on Spark; the first and last record by The Robins on the Atlantic subsidiary, Atco.

CHAPTER THREE

# THE COAST IS CLEAR

*'ATLANTIC LABELS IN CO-OP DEAL WITH SPARK FIRM. NEW YORK. NOV 12 1955*
*Atlantic records this week inked a many-faceted deal with Spark Associates, West Coast writing—publishing—talent—recording combine, consisting of Mike Stoller, Jerry Leiber, and Lester Sill. The Spark group, who operated the Spark label and Quintet music, have deactivated Spark and are turning over all masters to Atlantic. Stoller and Leiber, the song-writing team responsible for a number of hits, including "Black Denim Trousers", will write and acquire song material to be recorded for Atlantic and its subsidiary labels, which will be published in a new firm, Tiger Music, owned jointly by the Spark and Atlantic interests. Last year Stoller, Leiber, and Sill were reported on the verge of a similar deal with Decca, but this never materialized. Their negotiations with Atlantic began several weeks ago, when the latter purchased the Spark master of "Smokey Joe's Cafe" by The Robins, which is now doing well on the subsidiary Atco label. Already, new Stoller–Leiber tunes have been recorded by Atlantic's Joe Turner and Ruth Brown and have placed in Tiger Music. Atlantic plans also to reissue several Spark discs of last year which never received nationwide distribution on that label. The diskery has taken over artists' contracts with blues singers, Frankie Marshall and Garland the Great. The Robins group has broken up but Atco plans to build a new unit around the lead and bass singers.'*

Two months before *Billboard* ran that notice on 19 November, Nesuhi Ertegun was working in Los Angeles where he produced a session with Atlantic's foremost black vocal group, The Drifters. Ertegun was impressed by what he had heard of The Robins and, as Mike Stoller recalls, took a keen interest in the group: 'Nesuhi put us in touch with Atlantic in New York. Lester and Jerry went over there and set up a deal whereby Atlantic bought all the Spark masters and contracted us as producers to keep working with the group. I think that was the first independent production deal ever made. Our first issue on Atco was a re-release of "Smokey Joe's Cafe" and, with their distribution, instead of selling 90,000 copies we sold 250,000. Roy, Billy, and Terrell remained with their manager, then Gene Norman, who was starting a new record company and didn't want the group to come to Atlantic with us. This left Carl, who was fairly new to the group, and Bobby Nunn. Carl found replacements immediately and Lester Sill, who became their manager, called them The Coasters to identify them with the West Coast.'

Carl Gardner has also explained why he believes the split was necessary: 'The Robins were frightened of big deals, they were a little afraid of people. They had come way back y'know, long before I got started professionally and they were scared of signing contracts with people because they thought they'd get screwed around. They'd also gotten used to California. I left Texas looking for somethin' bigger than being with a group and, at the time, I was reluctant to stay with The Robins 'cos they wanted to stick around their wives. They would say, "Hey, man, I don't wanna travel" and what they meant was they wanted to stay with their families. I had just left my wife in Texas—and pregnant also—and I thought if I could do it, so can they. But it didn't work out like that and I went on with Leiber and Stoller... I always thought, "Right on Carl, straight ahead," forget about somebody screwing you around. I had the mind and I was taught by older musicians how to take care of myself when it came to royalty checks and things like that ... I tried to persuade The Robins to go along with the deal but half of 'em says, "No, I'm not gonna sign." I went ahead with Leiber and Stoller and I'm pleased I trusted 'em, very much so. You gotta trust somebody in this world. The Robins didn't sign up and they jus' went backwards.'

When Spark folded The Robins—suitably augmented—went to Whippet, a subsidiary of G.N.P. (Gene Norman Presents) with offices on the Sunset Strip. Initially, Carl Gardner was not entirely sure which group owned his services but he was soon given assistance in making up his mind: 'Y'know we was getting ready to record for Gene Norman, some little things, er "Cherry Lips" and "Out of the Picture, Out of the Frame". I was about to record those particular tunes when Leiber and Stoller walked in. Someone served a paper on me saying that they wanted me to record for them or they would get a lawyer because I was signed to them and had no business to be doing songs for Gene Norman. So I had to leave during the session, jus' as The Robins were cutting "Cherry Lips". Grady Chapman sang lead and the others, Billy, Roy and Terrell, were there. Y'know I may even be on it, I'm not sure.'

H. B. Barnum, an astute jack-of-all trades whose association with The Coasters was to recur again, produced every Robins' record cut for Whippet although none could be called essential. In March 1956, *Billboard* gave an 80 rating to 'Cherry Lips'—'a spirited, uninhibited vocal treatment of a stinging rhythm ditty with an excellent performance by the singers'—but it is hard to account for the reviewer's enthusiasm today. A slender novelty, 'Cherry Lips' has jerky rhythms which build around the noise made by one of the group kissing the back of his hand. 'Out of the Picture', a swinging close harmony song, would have been suitable for The Four Freshmen, while 'Hurt Me' is a big Platters-style ballad. Without Leiber and Stoller the group had, once again, lost every vestige of originality and distinctiveness. Whippet ceased to function after less than thirty issues but The Robins remained in Los Angeles where they continued to record for a number of small and equally short-lived independent labels. They had no more hits and, while some of their later sides are easily enjoyed, to say more than this would permit them an unwarranted importance.

Carl Gardner and Bobby Nunn found a second tenor, a baritone, and a guitarist within two weeks. 'Billy Guy lived opposite,' said Gardner. 'After I left The Robins I called on him and then I went to Bobby's house in Watts and he told me about Leon Hughes who sang a little bit. (Bobby Nunn: "Leon was a dancer and I didn't know whether he could sing or not but nonetheless I went and hauled him out of the car-wash where he worked—his voice turned out to be kinda weak."[1]) Leon wasn't the greatest but we needed somebody fast 'cos Leiber and Stoller wanted a quick session. Bobby was responsible for getting Adolph Jacobs together, he was a kid y'know—about eighteen—but he was playing guitar to the best of his ability. He was young and he was learning so we picked him up. We started a group from scratch and jus' said "Let it ride"—we never tried to find anybody who could sing, read, or play better than any other person. The first guys we asked came along in good friendship and that was it. Me, Leon Hughes, Billy Guy, Bobby Nunn, and Adolph Jacobs on guitar—the first group to record as The Coasters.'

Remaining in Los Angeles, The Coasters first session produced 'Brazil', 'Down in Mexico', 'One Kiss Led to Another', and 'Turtle Dovin' '. Gardner takes lead vocal on all four, sharing 'Brazil', a minor standard and something of a West coast r & b hit for saxophonist Lynn Hope (Aladdin 3229), with Bobby Nunn. A lyrically dull recollection of pleasures experienced there, 'Brazil' may, nonetheless, have been the first r & b record to have employed the kind of counterpoint heard, very much later, on the discs of Neil Sedaka and many of New York's girl groups. Gardner, his tenor soaring high above the simple layer of '. . . Old Brazil, down in old Brazil . . .' recalls thrills of love beneath a twilight sky. He sings as though he means every word but the general feel, bouncy arrangement, and lack of good humour was reminiscent of The Ray Conniff Chorus. It was not an experiment that Leiber and Stoller were moved to repeat. 'Brazil' is valuable only in providing the perfect low to the perfect high of 'Down in Mexico'. Mexicali lies 140 miles South East of Los Angeles just beneath the Mexican –American border. Guidebooks issued by The Southern Californian Visitors Council contain the enigmatic entry of 'bordertown pastimes' against the town. There is no further explanation; to find one pleasure-seekers can do no better than listen to the record which begins, in fact, 'A down in Mexicali there's a crazy little place that I know.' The drinks are hot, there's chili sauce to accompany the beans, and the boss is a cat named Joe. On this occasion, Joe reveals his split-personality; he now wears Mexican national costume, plays a blues piano and even offers friendly advice:

*'Well the first time that I saw him*
*he was a sittin' on a piano stool*
*I said "tell me dad when does the fun begin?"*
*he jus' winked his eye an' said "Man be cool".'*

The dancing girl is no less provocative and the singer accepts her invitation to dance without interruption from Joe. The climax to their relationship is disguised by the song's closing advice to anyone who might find themselves South of the border:

*'You wanna get straight—Man, don't hesitate*
*Jus' look up a cat named Joe.'*

'Down in Mexico'—like 'Smokey Joe's Cafe'—relies musically upon latin rhythms; the construction of each song is equally precise, and lyrically both draw upon the same source. 'Down in Mexico' made the r & b top ten without making any kind of dent in the national pop charts. Significantly, the remaining numbers from the same session reveal the very first indications that Leiber and Stoller were changing the content of their compositions, away from the adult black audience at which the records of The Robins had been aimed, towards a young, white audience who were developing a taste for black music providing it was called rock 'n' roll.

To a crisp, punchy accompaniment, 'Turtle Dovin'' celebrates a girl who is satisfied to do no more than that. She doesn't want to go to shows or put on fancy clothes and the singer has a lot of fun without spending a dime. A year later, Leiber and Stoller used the same idea for Elvis Presley's 'Baby I don't care', one of three numbers which, including the title, they wrote for the Avon–MGM film, 'Jailhouse Rock'. In the song, a girl who dislikes crazy music and rocking bands is deservedly rebuked for being 'square'. It's a nice idea but not in the same league as 'Turtle Dovin'' which retains a casual humour—'I hear the stop-work whistle blow/my work is done it's time to go'—sadly all to often absent from anything which Presley recorded after joining RCA-Victor. When Stoller said that 'Love Me' was the worst song he and Leiber had ever composed, he was forgetting 'Steadfast, Loyal and True'. This and some of the other Leiber–Stoller songs Presley recorded—'Love Me', 'Don't', 'Just Tell her Jim said Hello', 'Loving You', 'She's Not You'—are largely glucose ballads which differ little from what Leiber has described as 'the over-idealized songs spawned by Tin Pan Alley in the old days'.[2] But there were, of course, very good reasons for the comparative sterility of this material. The urban blues satire at which Leiber and Stoller were then so brilliant would only have miscast Elvis; the atmosphere at RCA's offices was not conducive to works of incisive wit ('It was like an insurance office,' said Stoller, 'all creativity and inspiration was drained immediately'); and they were further handicapped by the need to operate within the limits of Presley's incredibly stodgy film scripts ('You couldn't write a great piece of music for a purposely slushy *alma mater* and "Loving You" we wrote for a film; there were certain kinds of things asked for in those'). Despite these constraints, Leiber and Stoller managed to write a few of Presley's better post Sun records: 'Trouble' (magnificently earthy lines like 'My daddy was a green-eyed mountain jack') and 'Santa Claus is Back in Town' ('. . . no sleigh with reindeer, no sack on my back/you're gonna see me comin' in a big black Cadillac') are equal to any of their best compositions for The Coasters with whom, of course, no similar restrictions or difficulties occurred.

As in 'Turtle Dovin'', an essentially teenage occupation is also treated humorously in 'One Kiss led to Another', the only 'pop' hit to emerge from The Coasters' first session:

*'My girl-friend was a baby sittin' down the street,*
*an' so I bought some soda pop and sandwich meat*
*she laid it on the table an' I took a seat*
*but I never got a chance to drink or eat*
*'Cos one kiss led to another, and another, and another.* x 2

Like the 'chef-hat' and the 'stop-work whistle' it is impossible not to crack a smile at the mention of 'sandwich meat'. Unfortunately neither of these praiseworthy songs were issued outside the U.S.A. and Leiber and Stoller's growing preoccupation with juvenile activities is best explored in the light of records which are more accessible. The next session produced two—'Searchin'' and 'Young Blood'—which became available all over the world and a third recording—'Sweet Georgia Brown'—which failed to sell in either popular or r & b markets. Apart from producing the first of the group's enormous national hits, Mike Stoller remembers the session well. He was very lucky to be there; with the royalties which had accrued from the success of The Cheers' 'Black Denim Trousers', Stoller had taken a vacation in Europe and after a stay of three months, he and one thousand others embarked for the

U.S.A. on *The Andrea Doria.* Fifty-four passengers never arrived. On 25 July 1956 *The Andrea Doria* collided with a Swedish steamer, *The Stockholm*, near Nantucket Island and sank during the early hours of the morning. Survivors, including Stoller, were picked up by *The Cape Ann*, a fruit freighter from Bremerhaven, which headed for New York: 'Jerry was in New York for a convention and he was waiting on the dock with the whole Atlantic crew. It was the first time I had met Ahmet Ertegun, Jerry Wexler, Herb Abramson because Jerry and Lester had fixed the Spark deal while I stayed in L.A. Anyhow I was O.K. because I'd been taken off *The Andrea Doria* by a lifeboat. So we talked and then we went back to California to record The Coasters.'

Held in Los Angeles just over a year after The Coasters were formed, the second session was also attended by a fresh second tenor-cum-baritone. 'By the time we got around to "Searchin'" and "Young Blood",' recalled Stoller, 'Leon Hughes wasn't with them. I think he was probably sick. He had come into the group as a friend of Bobby Nunn's but he was the least musical person ever involved in The Robins or The Coasters and we replaced him with Young Jessie. Leon may still have been around but there are only four voices on the break-up of "Looka there" in "Young Blood" and Jessie is definitely one of those.' Like Richard Berry, Obediah 'Young' Jessie came from The Flairs with whom he sang baritone, and occasionally lead vocal, in 1954. He had also enjoyed, under his own name, three r & b hits, 'Mary Lou' (Modern 961), 'Hit, Git, and Split' (Modern 1002), and, a Leiber–Stoller composition, 'Here comes Henry' (Modern 1010). All three were exceptionally fine examples of early black rock 'n' roll but Jessie did not remain with The Coasters for much more than a year and his contribution to their own recordings, while perhaps greater than that of Leon Hughes, was nonetheless of minimal importance. On the other hand, Billy Guy, who shared lead vocal with Carl Gardner on 'Sweet Georgia

Brown', soon revealed just how valuable a recruit he really was.

Gardner's voice is conventional but distinctive. The ends of his words or phrases are frilled with an extra high note and many of his numbers, from his recordings with The Robins right up to the early seventies, are punctuated by exclamatory 'oohs' of similar pitch. This 'squeal', whether of anguish or delight, is a characteristic common to a number of Texan r & b singers including those, like Roy Brown and Eddie 'Cleanhead' Vinson, whose influence on Gardner was paramount. Tough blues, tender ballads or comic novelties held no special difficulty—Gardner is a safe, experienced, and versatile dance band singer whose vocal character can be said to owe a great deal to previous Texan styles. Billy Guy, however, does not appear to have borrowed from anybody. Ostensibly a rich baritone, he propelled his voice in whatever absurd, mangled direction Leiber and Stoller required; as a vocal comedian-cum-chameleon he has no equivalent in rock 'n' roll and few performances bear this out as much as 'Sweet Georgia Brown'. When the Richards brothers left The Robins, Carl had literally crossed the road to find a boy who 'sang a little bit'. He returned with Guy, a tall, gangling youth with long sideburns, a thin moustache, and a hoody process which tumbled down over his forehead: 'See, when I graduated high school,' said Guy, 'that was when Carl was with The Robins and they had jus' broke up. And it wasn't anything, it wasn't planned, I jus' fell into it becos' I lived across the street from him and he wanted to make a record but he didn't have nobody to do background. He jus' asked me if I wanted to sing on the record.'

On the first session, Guy does indeed sing 'background'; he sings the titles in unison and he 'oohs' and 'aahs' in all the right places—just one of the hired mouths. 'Sweet Georgia Brown' was a revelation to Leiber and Stoller, they could have combed Watts for years without finding a wizard like Guy. The record opens with Gardner taking four lines which could so easily have come from any of Leiber and Stoller's classics. He sings slowly and passionately—'Whooooh, a who's that chick in the yellow dress, well, well, well, well, well, well, well, a' that's the chick that I love best'—stretching all the phrases to include more than his usual quota of exclamations. Before Carl has finished Billy Guy comes in, shrieking and sorethroating his way through the bridge where he flies off in manic disregard for pitch, key, or meter. All three are variable. His voice fluctuates as if one's finger is periodically jabbing the turntable. And then the immortal line 'she gotta walk that make a hound dog talk', on which Guy simply overflows into the oft-repeated title where, as if overcome by his own performance, there is a kind of vocal detumescence as he subsides into his natural dark-brown voice. Leiber and Stoller must have seen the heavens opening. Here was a genuine comic who could do whatever they wished. He whined, screamed, chuckled, grunted, and cracked up. Moreover, he scarcely needed instructions. It was a role which he had been cultivating for the past three years.

Born in Attasca, Texas on 20 June 1936, Guy moved to Los Angeles with his family at the age of ten. By 1954 he had formed a comedy duo with Emmanuel Perez and recorded 'Ding Dong Ding' and 'Du-Tra-De-Du' (Aladdin 3287) as Bip and Bop: 'We worked high school gyms from, say San Francisco down to L.A., the whole coastline. To this day I don't know who was Bip and who was Bop, we never even thought about it. But in fact Emmanuel Perez was Mexican and we must have been one of the first integrated acts to hit L.A. That was a time we used to do all—you remember Gene and Eunice?—we sang their numbers, stuff like "Kokomo". But, it was funny, The Platters even copied after us. We came onstage an' we had two or three little tricks and The Platters were hu . . . ooooge but I looked around on TV and saw them doing the same performance. They had the nerve to come back and take—remember the thing we used to do with the legs? (imitates busker's trick of placing hands on opposite knees and rapidly switching them over to create the illusion of rubber joints)—me and 'Manuel we did that in The Oasis and I turned right around and The Platters were on TV doing our whole act! Still, I made more money with Bip and Bop than The Robins did with a lot of big records. They'd be with a lot of other groups, thrown together in a package and each getting fifteen to twenty dollars a night. With us the situation was different. Like here are only two guys playing fifteen high-schools all across the valley to San Francisco five nights a week. The Robins could have gone and sold eight million records but it was still no more'n 250 dollars a night onstage. Bip and Bop were having a ball and making ourselves 350 dollars week from the local schools.'

Billy Guy also sang lead on 'Searchin'', the first of The Coasters' songs to draw inspiration from the heroes of popular culture. It was not a common occurrence although other figures—Thelonius Monk (on 'Soul Pad'), The Beatles (on 'Wild One')—appear from time to time. 'Searchin'', however, lists a slew of mythical figures from the annals of criminal detection. Guy's voice is shrill and screechy, breaking into falsetto for additional comic effect. Sam Spade, Charlie Chan, Sherlock Holmes, Sgt. Joe Friday, and Bulldog Drummond are among the fictional sleuths whose names can be deciphered. Guy's expertise outshines them all, rivalling the motto of the Canadian Redcoat: 'But I'm like that North West Mountie, you know I'll bring her in someday.' That line came, virtually intact, from Mercy Dee Walton's 1954 blues, "Trailing my Baby" (Rhythm 1774) While Guy's voice registers appropriate determination, the most unusual innovation came from Mike Stoller who pumps out an insistent rhythm which Charlie Gillett has described as 'an alley piano style—essentially two bass notes, played alternately on every second beat'. It was extensively copied by a number of other Los Angeles writers and producers, notably H. B. Barnum, Fred Smith, and Gary Paxton, many of whose (yet to be discussed) group records combined shrill black voices with a simple refrain which echoed that of 'Searchin''. The song was on the popular best-selling record charts for over six months, a term which, among rock 'n' roll hits, was surpassed by less than half a dozen records. Incredibly, 'Young Blood', the reverse of 'Searchin'' was among them. The title, delicious in itself, was supplied by Doc Pomus: 'I had known of Doc for years,' recalled Stoller. 'He used to sing a commercial over the air for a pants shop in Brooklyn. Ali's Pants or Ali's Slacks, something like that. He'd sing it as a blues, y'know, "Ali, Ali you're so good to me . . ." I used to hear it on the Symphony Sid record show, a jazz programme, but he played a lot of blues and I remember Sid announcing, at the end of the commercial, "that was Doc Pomus with 'Ali's Slacks'". Now the title, "Young Blood" was passed on to us by Herb Abramson or Jerry Wexler who thought it was terrific. We took the title and we wrote the song. We decided that we would credit Doc as co-composer. It just happened that he didn't write any of the song but he's a capable writer and went on to compose a great many good songs with Mort Shuman. But in this particular case we didn't meet Doc; Jerry or Herb simply said "Doc Pomus has come up with this great title and I think it could be a winner."'

The seduction of a young girl by an older man is one of the commoner themes in both blues and rock 'n' roll. Elderly blues singers like Sonny Boy Williamson have seen nothing incongruous about singing 'Good morning little schoolgirl, can I go home with you?' Similar variations—'I want a little girl', 'Hey little girl', 'Hello little schoolgirl', The Robins 'Schoolgirl Blues'—are known to every blues and rock 'n' roll singer and the number of recorded versions on the same theme would fill a very thick ledger. Some, like 'Girl Fifteen' by Floyd Dixon (Aladdin 3069) and 'Jailbait' by Andre Williams (Fortune 837), warned of the dangers involved in following the proclivities of Sonny Boy Williamson, The Robins, and others. The Coasters paid no heed whatsoever. The girls in their songs are petite, luscious, precocious, and, by implication, white. There were exceptions—'Bigfoot Mae' ('The Idol with The Golden Head') and the Mississippi Momma in 'Soul Pad'—but they generally follow a juicy, comic-strip pattern; they have retroussé noses and big, round eyes; they wear tight sweaters and short skirts and they live on a diet of potato chips. They are also young. Some are very young indeed; lunchbreaks appear to have been invented for the paedophile's indulgence. Male teenagers clearly identified with the situation in which The Coasters were placed but the voices of the group betrayed an age at which an interest in young girls might be deemed decidedly unhealthy. In 'Gee Golly' we are informed, perhaps for safety's sake, that the pretty child with the knocked-out mouth has recently passed the age of consent. It is very often difficult to believe. They are followed home from school. They go roller-skating. They skip around in the park. They are invariably subject to parental disciplines. The girl in 'My Baby Comes to Me (when she wants good lovin')' is dependent upon her father for new shoes and 'she goes to see her mother when she's down and got the blues'; the listener is urged to 'Dance' indoors if 'her momma won't let you take her out' and the wayward tomboy of 'Ladylike' ought to be at home helping her mother instead of hanging around the blue-light diner which 'ain't no place for a girl or a minor'. An element of this last characteristic, a polarization between adults and teenagers, also occurs in 'Young Blood', the most lascivious of all 'girl-following' rock 'n' roll songs and the very pinnacle of male chauvinist piggery:

'I saw her standing on the corner, a yellow ribbon in her hair' ... The yellow ribbon has a flavour of innocence, a defenceless touch; the gloating observer is perhaps doubly mischievous. But he is not alone; three others drool over her brain-bending charms:

*'I couldn't keep myself from shouting "A looka there" looka there, eh heh looka there, a looka there.'*

Each echoes the lead singer's instruction. One growls, one

feigns goofiness, and another collapses, scarcely able to enunciate his words for chuckling over some evil if scarcely secret intention. The street corner letchers are totally besotted. Their agitation increases until they're barely able to keep their trousers on. Shucking, jiving, jeering, poking, lusting—the innuendo is so heavy you half expect a prophylactic to roll out of the sleeve:

*'I took one look an' I was fractured*
*I tried to walk but I was lame*
*I tried to talk but I just stuttered "What's your name"*
*What's your name, heh eh what's your name, a what's your name.'*

While the first refrain catalogues their various afflictions, the second shows blacks in the light of a potentially dangerous form of inadequacy:

*'I had to follow her all the way home*
*then things went bad—I met her dad*
*he said, "You better leave my daughter alone."'*

The immaturity of he who falls in love every day is also underlined by the concluding stanza which has a neat paradox and an amusing scenic reference:

*'Well I couldn't sleep a wink for trying*
*I saw the rising of the sun*
*an' all night long my heart was crying,*
*You're the one, you're the one, you're the one, you're the one.'*

Blues with a similar theme had long been enjoyed within the privacy of the black community but 'Young Blood' sold a million and crashed through all racial barriers. This and the general tenets of hits like it was responsible for much of the adult antagonism towards rock 'n' roll. White parenthood failed to appreciate songs by middle-aged blacks who relished the idea of importuning adolescent girls in the street. Committed segregationalists launched a vigorous attack. The savage music and idiotic words of black rock 'n' roll records were said to undermine the moral fibre of the nation's white children. Above the Mason–Dixon line, whites were not seriously impressed by such claims but they remained puzzled by lyrics they thought incomprehensible or insistent upon love which was impetuous or transitory but rarely eternal. The slurred or mumble-worded approach of many r & b vocal groups merely added fuel to the charge that such records were educationally destructive. There is no indication that Leiber and Stoller leapt to rock 'n' roll's defence. Via their chief interpreters, Presley and the inarticulate dimbo who persistently crops up in the songs of The Coasters, they could afford to take some of the blame. Instead, in 1958—in strong contrast to more recent interviews in *Fusion, Melody Maker, et al.*—they offered *Time* magazine a rare but disturbing gobbet of news: 'Kids nine to fourteen make up our market, we're tired of writing rock 'n' roll, but we can't stop.' Now lionized for perhaps creating the most dazzling of all commercial rock 'n' roll records, the heresy is softened, if not retracted. They could have been misquoted anyway.

With the success of 'Searchin'' and 'Young Blood', Atco issued an album containing seven old Robins' tracks and seven by the Coasters including only one new cut, 'Lola', the story of which is, to say the least, unusual. Mike Stoller: 'We first made that song with Bob London on Spark. Bob was a little short white singer, an imitation of Tony Martin, who pencilled in his receding hairline and probably sang with one of those big dance orchestras in the forties. We recorded him on two sides with a baion rhythm, "Lola" and "Reckless", and we held rehearsals in my house in L.A. with Carmen Miranda's old rhythm section, Joe Carioca on a small Brazilian guitar, Harry, a blond Brazilian, played percussion, and Fafa who played a fiddle. They were working in a restaurant down on Sunset Boulevard; they only read music a little but they learnt fast. Now most of our records had a red label but we put Bob London out on a blue label because that was gonna be our pop record as opposed to our r & b stuff. We shipped about a thousand records and we got back over a thousand. Samples came back as well. Then Ronnex records in Belgium asked for it and it became number one record of the year over there. Even "Reckless", the other side, was number five. It was reissued on Dot in the States but it still didn't do anything here. That was the original of The Coasters song; by the time we did the first Coasters dates we needed more sides for the first album. Although it included Robins songs we still didn't have enough so we had The Coasters sing "Lola" with Carl taking lead.' Bobby Nunn also takes a verse while Carl feigns a West Indian accent, 'Lola dunces in de market place.' Understandably, Carl could not recall making the song which is a truly abysmal listening experience.

'My Baby comes to Me,' recorded in New York's Capitol Studios in June 1957, had an uncharacteristically hackneyed set of lyrics ('She goes to see the doctor when she's got a cold / she goes to see the gypsy when she wants her fortune told'), and, although a reference to Coca-Cola confirms, once again, the age group at which it was aimed, the melody, a foolish replica of 'Searchin'', cannot have impressed anyone who listened. The weakest Coasters recording to date, it was issued on the reverse of a minor classic, 'The Idol with The Golden Head'. This and yet another splendid social satire, 'What is the secret of your success', were recorded in Chicago with highly respected black session musicians like Louis Myers and Freddy Below. 'The Coasters,' said Stoller, 'were having enormous success with "Searchin'" and "Young Blood". Around summer '57 they were in Chicago on the road and we grasped the opportunity to record at the Chess studios. It was really weird, a very difficult session indeed. We had some great blues musicians but they weren't familiar with the songs and they couldn't figure out where the changes were gonna be. As a matter of fact "What is the secret of your Success" is made up of two different takes in two different keys and that's how come you got that weird chord progression. At the end of each verse it slides up a half-tone; it wasn't originally written like that but we chopped it up afterwards. We flew into Chicago for three days, worked hard at Chess and then I think we chopped up the tapes when we got back to L.A.'

The song is one of Leiber and Stoller's unheralded goodies. Billy Guy is bewildered and exasperated by the good fortune of a smooth, sharp and cool character who drives a Rolls-Royce, smokes fat cigars and dates a movie starlet every night of the week:

> *'In all the fancy places they've heard of your fame,*
> *they bring the bill an' you just sign your name*
> *when you crack a joke everybody laughs*
> *all the girls are beggin' for your autograph*
> *You done tore up the country from East to West*
> *What is the secret of your success?'*

To the assertion that 'you bin able to achieve what a most folks cain't', the affluent Nunn throws in a line of smug complacency: 'Some cats got it and—er some cats ain't.' A contrast to 'Whadaya want' and a fore-runner of 'What about us', it's the joke of poverty again. Undeniably funny but, in a sense, it goes deeper. The jokes have the stoic and often painful pay-off which distinguishes those of this singer's troubled race. Issued as the b-side of 'Sweet Georgia Brown', it was far from successful but 'Idol with the Golden Head' soon re-established the group half-way up the *Billboard* Hot Hundred. The song appears to portray the effect of rock 'n' roll upon a middle-aged superstitious black from the Deep South. If this interpretation sounds fanciful it no more than matches the surrealistic lyric which has a number of particularly humorous stanzas. Between each line, spat out by Carl Gardner, the group maintain a repetitive chant while Freddy Below thrashes a terrific staccato back-beat from his kit:

*'Bought myself an idol with the golden head*
*put it on the shelf right above my bed.'*

The purchase, a telepathic totem, informs his owner of his girl-friend's whereabouts. It speaks with the same idiomatic use of the English language as any of Leiber's less mystical characters:

*'The idol's eyes began to wink and blink,*
*he said "Hold on Jim, give me time to think"*
*The lightning flashed and the idol did speak*
*he said, "Your Bigfoot Mae she's down in Catfish Creek".'*

Mae apparently retires to Catfish Creek to indulge in rock 'n' roll. The singer is thoroughly disturbed by news of her secret addiction and his hair turns grey when he goes off to Catfish Creek and surprises her in mid-frenzy. Finally, the idol advises Jim to overcome his irrational fears and bring himself up to date. He's told that he must learn to do the boogie with his Bigfoot Mae. Maybe it was some kind of answer to adult paranoia. Whatever sparked off Jerry Leiber, the record is certainly one of the finest in rock 'n' roll history and would have sold a million or more had The Coasters been able to promote it: 'We never did the record on stage,' said Bobby Nunn. 'Carl just couldn't sing that high normally and he was afraid of doing it live. In the studio Leiber and Stoller had a tendency to push you a little bit further than you can go. We flew to New York to do "Idol with the Golden Head" on The Patti Page Show but Carl didn't dare try and do it when we got there. We had to sing "Searchin'" instead.'[3]

In December, the group returned to the Capitol studios and recorded two straightforward rock 'n' roll songs,

'Dance' and 'Gee Golly', both unremarkable celebrations of teenage experience. 'Dance' advised that to win her heart and soul 'all you got to do is play some rock 'n' roll'. For 'Gee Golly', expressions of disbelief greeted a "Rockin' an' rollin' machine" who drove all the schoolboys wild. It was a thin idea which Billy Guy's adenoidal vocal failed to enhance and both songs lacked tension as well as rib-tickling lines. While Atlantic's session files and the re-allocated matrix numbers contradict each other, Mike Stoller believes that 'Wait a Minute' was recorded at the same time although not released until several years had passed. A harmless bit of nonsense about a guy who can't stand to hear his girl talking about other boys, it was written by Bobby Darin whose own self-composed hit 'Splish Splash' (Atco 6117), showed a far stronger individual humorist at work. Nonetheless, Billy Guy's braying lead was still sufficient a novelty to make 'Wait a Minute' one of The Coasters last big hits of 1961. In 1957 however, two—possibly three—unexceptional cuts from one session seemed like an unfortunate, if temporary, setback. Some fresh material, written well away from the stifling atmosphere in the RCA and Hill and Range offices where Leiber and Stoller had worked on first arriving in New York, was soon forthcoming. It was not the only reappraisal. A significant change in recording studios, the addition of a charismatic saxophone player and two vitally important personnel shuffles also helped to create a solid gold stream of indelibly memorable smash hits.

'I seem,' said Stoller, 'to remember Young Jessie and Bobby Nunn leaving the group and Cornel Gunter and Dub Jones coming in together. There was probably some kind of hassle and Jessie decided he wanted to stay in California and work with another group, continue perhaps with whatever Richard Berry was doing.' Carl Gardner has also described how Nunn, with his first taste of big money in ten years, decided to follow his friend, Leon Hughes, into retirement: 'Leon split before "Searchin'". He was married an' had about seven or eight kids. He had just gotten a big fat royalty cheque an' he says "Man, I'm going home." When Bobby's cheque came it was maybe 15,000 dollars an' he says, "I'm going too." He was married with one son and he says, "Man, I quit." It was on a one-nighter in Cleveland—I said, "15,000 dollars ain't gonna last you two minutes, you goin' home, you gonna buy yourself a Cadillac an' I say in three or four years I'll be back in L.A., an' you'll knock on my door an' ask for five dollars," an' he did an' I had to let him have five dollars.'

Gunter and Jones remained with The Coasters for five and nine years respectively. They both grew up in an area of Los Angeles where, in 1953, Dootsie Williams encountered what he described as a 'family of singers' who practised together: 'They all had different groups, all knew each other and would help each other but they were also stealing each other's material. Jesse Belvin was really the spark of that whole culture of fifteen to twenty guys.'[4] The fraternity, larger than Williams' recollection, included The Medallions (Vernon Green, Randolph Bryant, Willie Graham, Ira Foley), The Dootones, The Meadowlarks (Don Julian, Ronald Barrett, Glenn Reagan, Earl Jones), The Turks, The Penguins (Cleveland Duncan, Dexter Tisby, Bruce Tate, Curtis Williams), an embryonic Platters, and, of course, The Flairs led by Cornel Gunter who, with Belvin, is one of the little-known but nonetheless seminal influences on early Los Angeles group culture.

Born in Los Angeles on 14 November 1938, Gunter formed The Flairs from among his class-mates at Jefferson High. A demonstration tape for John Dolphin (subsequently issued as two sides by the group under the name of The Hollywood Blue Jays) brought the quintet to the attention of The Bihari brothers who, in June 1953, signed them up and, according to Gunter, named Flair, their new subsidiary r & b label, after the group. While they remained popular on the West Coast throughout the fifties, the Flairs were fated to remain on small labels where, apart from the odd r & b top ten regional hit, they never enjoyed wide appeal. But of all the many Californian r & b groups, few contained so many talented individuals (three of whom—Richard Berry, Obediah Jessie, and Cornel Gunter—played various roles in the careers of The Robins and The Coasters) and, in the development of groupdom, The Flairs undoubtedly deserve a chapter to themselves. Their manager, songwriter Buck Ram, whose firm, Personality Promotions, also handled The Platters and The Penguins, has described how The Flairs were much the best of all his acts and why, in comparison to some of the others, they achieved so little fame: 'They were my favourite group believe me. 17- or 18-year-old kids, they were so fresh and so energetic and so perfectly in tune. Cornel Gunter is particularly interesting; he had actually started The Platters and given them that name before forming The Flairs who were already together and recording for Modern records when they came to me. Being so young they had nothing to do except go to school or rehearse. They were really dedicated but they never got the breaks like The Platters because I couldn't get them on a major label. Y'see The Platters were on Mercury which was really a running company, boy the minute they smelled a hit they covered all the disc-jockeys, they really knew what to do with the satchel. "Only You" was a big hit overnight but even after The Platters hit, everybody knew The Flairs had it better. They danced better, sang better, and their records were much funkier. But Modern was strictly a race label and, although they had a lot of r & b hits, they could never get played on pop stations. Modern couldn't go to a pop disc-jockey and pay him like they could with the r & b jocks, there was far more intrigue involved. Nonetheless, I tried really hard to break The Flairs: I worked through Modern's studios with the fine arranger, Maxwell Davis, and we used The Platters formula—that modified Inkspots sound, a heavy drumbeat and piano triplets—on a number of things including "Headin' Home" (Modern 989), which was done with Cornel's sister,

Shirley Gunther, singing lead. We could have had a white pop smash with that if Modern had worked on it but the publisher gave it to Della Reese who made an atrocious job of it.

'There wasn't a great deal of respect for these kids. California is very bad—you can't sign an artist who is under age unless you get parental permission and get it certified in court and The Flairs were being taken for a ride. The Bihari brothers epitomized the rock 'n' roll business as we knew it. They were tough and rugged and they knew how to grab the money while The Flairs were scared, under-privileged, and straight off the streets. The Biharis had them recording under all sorts of names (The Hunters, The Whips, The Five Hearts, The Rams) and they weren't getting paid for it. It was a practice they had and it rubbed off on the performers: while Cornel was under contract to me, he went off and signed The Flairs over to Zeke Manners at Loma. The record came out as The Ermines and I didn't know a thing about it until I recognized his voice on the air. Now if Cornel had managed himself properly he would have been as big as Little Richard, I firmly believe he had the talent but there aren't many people who could put up with his gags—he still goes around telling everybody that his mother wrote all of my songs.'

Before joining The Coasters, Gunter also found time to cover Sam Cooke's 'You Send Me' (Dot 15654), record other solo sides for Eagle and Liberty and spread some more stories. Like Little Richard, he never failed to embellish or distort history and most assertions—to have recorded with The Platters he mentions the Mercury hit 'The Magic Touch'), to have recorded for Motown, to have sung lead on all The Coasters hits—can be ignored. The claim to have played piano (he also plays vibes and organ) on America's favourite oldie, The Penguin's 'Earth Angel', may have more substance but it's hard to tell.

As bass with The Cadets, Will 'Dub' Jones had also sold a lot of records before joining The Coasters. A five strong, multi-faceted group with a triple identity, The Cadets—Aaron Collins, Willie Davis, Ted Taylor, Ron Townson (or George Hollis) and Jones—made rock 'n' roll cover versions for Modern as themselves; accompanied pianist—singer Jimmy Beasley as The Rockets; recorded ballads for RPM as The Jacks and backed up pop singer, Paul Anka, for the same label. The Cadets are best remembered as The Biharis West Coast equivalent of The Charms covering a host of hit records including Nappy Brown's 'Don't be Angry' (956), The Willow's 'Church Bells May Ring' (985), and Presley's 'Heartbreak Hotel' (985), all of which failed to improve on the original. Their luck changed with 'Stranded in the Jungle' (994); a top twenty hit in August 1956, it surpassed sales of The Jayhawks' previous recording. One of the most entertaining of all rock 'n' roll novelties, it begins with exotic and nocturnal sounds behind Dub Jones' effectively sour narration. The refrain cuts in like two different records spliced together, a technique used by Buchanan and Goodman, white comedians who enjoyed a series of successful novelty records during the same year. As the classic, oft-parodied rock 'n' roll backbeat fades out, Dub returns with a spoken verse which weds technology to a more primitive idea. Composed by James Johnson, lead tenor with The Jayhawks, the lyric is very nearly worthy of Jerry Leiber; read on and smile.

*'The boys in the jungle had me on the run,*
*when somethin' heavy hit me like an atomic bomb*
*when I woke up and my head started to clear*
*ah had a strange feeling ah was wid cookin' gear*
*ah smelled somethin' cookin' an' ah looked to see*
*that's when ah found out they was er cookin' me.'*

Follow-ups to 'Stranded in the Jungle', included 'Dancing Dan' (1000), another variant on Billy Ward's influential 'Sixty Minute Man', several standards and even a calypso but the Cadets had no more hits. Dub Jones and lead tenor, Aaron Collins, both of whom received featured billing on a number of these performances, also shared lead on most of the material. The slower songs which Collins preferred are not the forum in which Jones could be most distinctive but 'Why don't you write me' (RPM 428), a hit for the same group as The Jacks in 1955, is exceptional. A pretty ballad, Jones' bass doo-wahs nonetheless kick the song all the way home; where he takes the lead as in 'Hands Across The Table' (Modern 1024) or 'Stranded in The Jungle', he confirms that he is one of the finest bass singers that group r & b had to offer. When The Cadets split up in 1957, Aaron Collins and Willie Davis joined The Flares (Buck Ram had changed the spelling to avoid a lawsuit against an instrumental combo calling themselves The Flairs), Ted Taylor embarked on a long solo career and Dub Jones joined The Coasters where his frequent, one-line, fool-guy interjections soon became more than crucial to the group's sound.

Carl Gardner (lead tenor), Billy Guy (lead baritone), Cornel Gunter (second tenor), and Dub Jones (bass): this, to even the most casual admirer, was the most significant of all The Coasters' personnel. It is this permutation which is heard on all their internationally known hit records and that most commonly seen in publicity portraits of the group. There was also a 'fifth' Coaster—the late King Curtis—who played on all their subsequent New York recordings and even produced a couple of sides when Leiber and Stoller lost interest. 'We met King on some other record sessions,' said Stoller. 'I can't recall which but I asked him to take the first Coasters date at Atlantic's new studios. King was a fantastic musician and he was great to work with because he knew almost instantaneously what we were looking for.'

Born in Fort Worth, Texas on 7 February 1934, Curtis—whose real name was Curtis Ousley—became the only rock 'n' roll saxophonist to enjoy anything like household name status. His father, who played guitar in church, discouraged his interest in jazz but Curtis had heard Louis Jordan's alto saxophone on the radio and wanted to play the instrument more than anything else in the world. His father relented and bought him one in 1945. Curtis switched to tenor during high school and—before returning to Texas with the offer of a musical scholarship—he won an amateur night talent contest at The Apollo on a visit to relatives in New York. Studies uncompleted, he led his own combo around Texas clubs. By 1958 when, like The Coasters, he was contracted to Atco, he had played with Lionel Hampton's band, formed a jazz trio with Horace Silver and Osie Johnson, and recorded under his own name for many independents including Gem, Crown, Apollo, and Groove. Yet, apart from the odd prestige jazz session, Curtis was not an improvisor. Nor, unlike Herb Hardesty with Fats Domino, any of Little Richard's horn-men or even Jimmy Wright with The Teenagers, is there any record of Curtis playing on his back, shoulders heaving like pistons, blowing the reed out of his instrument. Prior to deployment as a freelance studio musician, he had followed a fairly uneventful career in the mainstream footsteps of Lester Young, Arnett Cobb, and Gene Ammons to whom he would always refer when interviewed. Unlike the apoplectic honkers of the period (who could rarely be distinguished from one another), Curtis brought a readily identifiable tone to whatever he played, be it blues (where he accompanied Sunnyland Slim and Roosevelt Sykes), r & b influenced pop (Sam Cooke, Little Eva, Bobby Darin, Sammy Turner) or jazz (Nat Adderley, Wynton Kelly), the medium he much preferred until the early sixties when he discovered his forte lay in the warm soul ballad style which Southern soul singers had brought to Atlantic around that time. Within each of these categories, he was not only prolific but versatile. His solos on records by Sammy Turner are light years away from his tricky embellishments with The Coasters but they are still natural, effortless and unmistakably King Curtis. While he despised anything quite so rudimentary as honking away on one note and rarely indulged in any obvious commitment to excitement, rock 'n' roll tenor playing was left firmly in the diaphragms of Sil Austin or Red Prysock, neither of whom were especially valuable to record companies who sought session men who could play whatever was required of them. At this, Curtis had unparalleled skills: 'He did exactly what we said,' recalled Stoller, 'Jerry and I would write the saxophone parts which repeat themselves between phrases and we would tell King exactly what we wanted the solos to be. Y'know, sometimes Jerry would be whispering in his ear while he was playing, singing little phrases to him during the solo break.' The buzz-saw phrases of Gil Bernal or Plas Johnson had their own appeal. Like the walls of 'Smokey Joe's Cafe', they were dirty, coarse, and greasy. King Curtis was clean, note-perfect and his solo breaks on The Coasters' records have no equivalent in rock. His tone—deep, fruity, and round with a characteristic burr that slides into a growl or stutter—and his facility—memorably impressive figures and inflections—combine in under twenty seconds to create a unique statement full of charm and utility not once but over and over again. All the classics have it starting with 'Zing went The Strings of My Heart', the first of The Coasters songs to be recorded at Atlantic's 'new' studios on 234 West 56th Street.

'It was really an office,' said Stoller. 'Prior to our arrival they had just moved from 56th Street to 57th Street and before that the premises doubled as a studio and an office. When they wanted to record, they would move the chairs out of the way and pile one desk on top of another and then go ahead. When they moved to 57th Street, they kept the old office as a studio so they wouldn't have to stack the furniture up before they could do a session. It was an old kinda funky brownstone building with a very slow elevator that creaked it's way up to the fifth floor. The studio had a skylight in it and theoretically everything was wrong with it except the engineer, Tommy Dowd, who's a genius. We cut

"Zing went the Strings of my Heart", "Three Cool Cats", and "Yakety Yak" on an eight-track recorder. They were the first records of any note to be cut on an eight-track.'

It may cause a few faint snickers but 'Zing went the Strings of my Heart' really is a classic. Not the most inherently beautiful song ever written, it's just the sort of thing to send anyone under thirty-five reaching for the Alka Seltzer. Leiber and Stoller may have despised the idealistic sentiments of Tin Pan Alley but you wouldn't think so from this production. It embodies the highest conception of the most sophisticated 'bird' styled groups with all the freshness and crispness that 1958 studio techniques could muster. Moreover, no one sings with the slightest trace of a wink or a nod. In fact, the idea itself, a duet between Gunter and Jones, was redolent of The Inkspots who sang similarly romantic songs in a pleasant if fairly conventional manner, twenty years before. Jones takes the verses in his vibrant bass—infinitely richer and more satisfying than the monotone of Bobby Nunn—while Gunter, who soars in on the bridge, reveals a sonorous tenor, high, melismatic and as pure as cut glass. He never performed quite so beautifully before or since. He may well have been the finest lead singer The Coasters ever recruited but, as Carl Gardner has explained, a voice that could transform a corny song into a breath-taking experience was not necessarily the sort of voice that could also provoke laughter: 'Now Cornel sings beautifully; he's more than a little gay but he could really sing his head off. Now Leiber and Stoller were into this novelty stuff and the novelty things were tailored to suit Billy Guy and myself. I would say that we were the essence of that sound. Cornel was far from being a novelty personality and—it's a shame—because he wanted to do more things but Leiber and Stoller just didn't have room for a lead like that.'

Instead Leiber and Stoller re-embarked on a path from which the comic tradition in American rock has never entirely recovered. What would ghoulish, social satirist Shel

Silverstein have done without Leiber and Stoller's sensibilities to guide him? Who would find Sha Na Na more than an empty belly-laugh without the ironies of 'Yakety Yak'? Theatrically—as well as racially—the black humour of rock 'n' roll starts here. Leiber and Stoller had made nuggets before but the world did not become fully aware of them or The Coasters until 'Yakety Yak' topped the best-sellers on both sides of The Atlantic.

CHAPTER FOUR

# HOODLUM FRIENDS OUTSIDE

WHITES have generally thought of the black minority in terms of a Hollywood stereotype Stepin Fetchit image. According to sociologist John Dollard, in *Caste and Class in a Southern Town,*[1] the black man appeared as a 'lower class Negro, whining, vacillatory, shambling, stupid and moved by very simple cravings'. As a description of the black man in the songs of Jerry Leiber and Mike Stoller it seems to me that Dollard's collection of adjectives can scarcely be bettered. An examination of all The Coasters' songs reveals very powerfully a black sub-culture in which little work is done; where life is spent in pursuit of idle pleasures and where ridicule and oppression are accepted with a passive discontent.

The Coasters are exclusively concerned with working class contexts. Blue-light diners ('Ladylike'), docks and warehouses ('Bad Detective'), race-tracks ('Stewball'), pawnshops ('Run Red Run', 'My Baby comes to Me'), one-room shacks ('What about Us'), street-corners ('Young Blood', 'Three Cool Cats'), bars ('Tain't Nothin' to Me', 'I'm Sorry but I'm gonna have to pass'), alleys ('The Shadow Knows'), and laundromats ('Yakety Yak') amplifies the list which appeared in Chapter Two. The characters they portray or sing about are equally sure to be engaged in tawdry, menial, if not criminal occupations. A strip-tease dancer in 'Little Egypt'; a factory-hand in 'Turtle Dovin' '; a gypsy in 'Love Potion No. 9'; a private detective in 'Bad Detective'; a wino in 'D. W. Washburn', or a refuse-collector 'bound to his garbage truck' in 'Wake Me, Shake Me'. 'Sweeping up' is a 'good job' according to the narrator of 'Shopping for Clothes'. Other characters exhibit a whole cataract of antisocial values. Hard work, authority and many other 'white' ethics are resented while examples of vulgarity, dishonesty, or vagrancy abound. Almost every primitive characteristic to have been ascribed to blacks in general is to be found within the lyrics of The Coasters songs, particularly the alleged devotion to basic appetites. Food ('Hungry'); drink ('I'm sorry but I'm gonna have to pass'); gambling ('Run Red Run'), and an obsessive concentration on sex are well-documented. Combinations of all these hedonistic 'vices', and many more besides, occur in numerous songs. 'Red' of the last-cited title 'taught that monkey how to guzzle beer and taught him how to play stud-poker'. 'I'm a hog for you baby, can't get enough of your love' conveys a feeling of both food and sex in the single metaphorical declaration, an idea which is repeated in 'Down Home Girl' whose perfume smells like turnip greens and kisses taste like pork and beans. Whites could be excused for believing that blacks think of nothing else but it was not the only misconception Leiber and Stoller had occasion to reinforce. Bobby Nunn strengthened the myth of the black man's extraordinary genital development by boasting of the prowess of his 'chopper' in 'Hatchet Man'. If the black man is thought to be prone to over-excitability, Billy Guy adds credence to the impression by tearing his clothes when the horse he has backed in 'Stewball' looks like winning by a neck. Similarly, if the black man is considered untrustworthy, the potential confidence trickster who attempts to obtain pecuniary advantage by deception in 'Shopping for Clothes' does little to subvert the belief. The girl in 'Bad Blood' is a mean, promiscuous, inveterate liar but her entire family is equally corrupt; her mother and brother exhibit equally negative traits while her cousin is imprisoned down in Tennessee. Leiber and Stoller wrote thirteen songs for The Robins and thirty-seven for The Coasters. No more than a handful are entirely free from an interpretation which is derogatory to black people. They are shown to be sex mad ('Young Blood', 'One Kiss', 'Girls, Girls, Girls') to the point of profanity as well as promiscuity:

*'I'm sittin' in church on Sunday prayin' for a better life,*
*but I can't take my eyes off the Deacon's pretty wife'*
('Everybody's Woman')

They are also stupid and superstitious ('Idol with the Golden Head'); itinerant ('Keep on Rollin'') and—in many ways, the most damaging indictment of all from a Puritanical point of view—they simply never stop whining about the conditions they have to put up with—('What is the Secret of your Success', 'Yakety Yak', 'Charlie Brown', 'What about Us').

A song of novel construction—in so far as the title appears as a throwaway comment at the end of each verse—'Yakety Yak' is, *prima facie*, an indictment of the predictably boring and unnecessarily trivial responsibilities of adulthood. Stuck in a rut of routine household chores, adults can do no more than mock, scoff at, or threaten to curtail those youthful pleasures—pocket money, aimlessly riding around, rock 'n' roll itself—to which no such responsibilities are attached. On this level alone it is the best of the numerous rock 'n' roll songs to have helped define and formalize the generation gap which other factors—early sexual maturity, greater teenage affluence and prolonged schooling with increased leisure—had helped to create. '"Yakety Yak,"' explained Stoller, 'was really the first song that had to do with children, with teenagers so to speak. I don't know how consciously it was angled in that direction because I remember writing that with Jerry and Jerry shouted out the first line and I shouted the second line right back at him. I started playing piano and we wrote the song—the rest of the lyrics are Jerry's—from there, very rapidly.'

*Take out the papers an' the trash*
*or you don't get no spending cash*
*if you don't scrub that kitchen floor*
*you ain't gonna rock and roll no more.*

*Yakety Yak, don't talk back.*

*Just finish cleaning up your room*
*let's see that dust fly with that broom*
*get all that garbage out of sight*
*or you don't go out Friday night.*

*Yakety Yak, don't talk back.*

*You just put on your coat and hat*
*an' walk yourself to the laundromat*
*an' when you finished doin' that*
*bring in the dog and put out the cat.*

*Yakety Yak, don't talk back.*

*Don't you give me no dirty looks*
*your father's hip he knows what cooks*
*just tell your hoodlum friend outside*
*you ain't got time to take a ride.*

*Yakety Yak, don't talk back.*

'Yakety Yak' is an extraordinary list of instructions and threats. In the circumstances of its period, it is easy to conceive that a part of the record-buying audience embraced this persistent whine as indicative of something close to generational revolt rather than a simple, trenchant and witty expression of mere adolescent protest. For his part, Jerry Leiber claimed that: 'The Coasters appealed greatly to white kids because a lot of the material—pieces like "Charlie Brown" and "Yakety Yak"— really were slices of middle-class white teenage life. They're not black-oriented in terms of subject matter.'[2]

However, although the white American middle class may well use laundromats and refer to rubbish as 'trash' or 'garbage', what are we to make of 'Your father's hip, he knows what cooks'?

The imagination fails to accommodate a white, middle-aged, middle-class mother describing the awareness of her spouse in terms which are sprinkled with what is essentially Negro slang. Perhaps it's unfair to dissect Leiber's remarks out of context and it should be recorded that his partner saw the influence of black expression on white teenagers as a steady historical development: 'I guess there are some touches of the kinda things that we had done before that were, of course, very much involved with black culture. We can't have been the only white kids to have been involved with black people or black music when we wrote our first things together although we didn't know any others. But by the time "Yakety Yak" was written in 1957 so many—already by that time—so many white kids were getting into that.'

'Charlie Brown' poses the same question of which came first, the song or the audience—though perhaps more obliquely. Leiber and Stoller did not compose many songs about school situations. 'Gee Golly' is a catalogue of lustful exclamations aimed at a girl who walks 'through the school yard after school' but 'Snake and The Bookworm' was written by Doc Pomus and Mort Shuman and the pathetic 'PTA' ('when the parents finally get back, a lot of kids are gonna get a smack') was written by the white pop singer Paul Evans. When Frank Zappa parodied high school ethic in 'Status Back Baby' he could only have been prompted by 'Charlie Brown' to make the curious reference in the second stanza: 'The other night we painted posters, they played some records by The Coasters.'

'Charlie Brown' is a classically brief (and too predictable to be really funny) story of a dull, gormless youth; the group enumerate Charlie's particularly feeble attacks on authority while the bass voice gives expression to his wholly unbelievable innocence.

*'Fi Fi, Fie, Fie, Fo Fo Fum*
*I smell smoke in the auditorium*

*Charlie Brown, Charlie Brown*
*He's a clown, that Charlie Brown*
*He's gonna get caught, just you wait an' see*
*Why's everybody always pickin' on me.*

*That's him on his knees, I know that's him*
*Yellin' "Seven come eleven" down in the boy's gym*

*Who's always writing on the wall*
*Who's always goofin' in the hall*
*Who's always throwin' spitballs*

*Yes you—who me?—Yeah you.*

*Who walks in the class-room cool and slow*
*who calls the English teacher "Daddy-O".'*

Who has never written on the wall or goofed in the hall, possibly used a pea-shooter as well? Simple-minded non-conformism is to be found within every youngster, in every class, in every school, among every race of people. But who, even given that the opening line of the song suggests the alien Giant of white Jack and his beanstalk, walks in the 'cool and slow' gait peculiar to blacks? The mannerism was swiftly imitated by rebellious white teenagers but few who listen to Dub Jones whining, wheedling, subservient tone of voice would imagine that he portrayed a white youth or even a Pachuco. 'The trouble with most of Leiber and Stoller's songs,' wrote Charlie Gillett, 'is that they describe improbable or incongruous situations and get too many of their laughs from making black clowns out of the singers.'[3] Put another way 'Why is everybody always pickin' on me?' begs a very uncomfortable question. How many of the million middle-class white kids who bought 'Charlie Brown' were inclined to reply 'because stupid black kids are good for a laugh'?

Johnny Otis was upset by Leiber and Stoller's prediliction, from the beginning of their collaboration, to show blacks in an unflattering light: 'I was in a record distributors in LA seeing about some record we had, when these young kids walked in. Someone told them who I was and they came up and told me that they were songwriters and that they'd like to submit some material. What they did, they wrote the songs and brought them to me and I would change a line I thought was objectionable, or add a line or re-write the thing and I would become co-writer. There was a song called "Mainliner" for Little Esther on Federal, "Candle's Burnin' Low" for Mel Walker on Mercury (8295) and of course "Hound Dog". There was stuff in there that was objectionable because it was—they didn't know it—but it was something that would have been insulting to black people like shooting dice, razor cutting, and drinking gin or some crap like that. So I took it out. There were a number of others like that. I don't want to point the finger of guilt unduly at them. They weren't racist in the true sense of the word but they dwelled entirely on a sort of street society. It's a very fine point—sure, the artist who performed and created these things, that's where he was, he wasn't a family person going to a gig, he was in the alleys, he was out there in the street trying to make it with his guitar. But while it might be a true reflection of life it's not invariably a typical reflection of the typical life in the black community. Take "Charlie Brown", which alludes to a black hoodlum who's a clown in school. Sure, I know guys like that, but it's still a blanket stereotype of black people.

'The fact is, blues is a black art form and, until now, when it's been done it's been done by a black person. White people can interpret the blues but they didn't create them—they couldn't—it's something that grew out of the black community. This is well-known, a foregone conclusion. So the fact that a blues, the psychology of a blues, can apply to a white person or to anyone else doesn't excuse what they did because we know that it points specifically to the black community. I've been guilty, unconsciously guilty—I wrote a song for Rucker recently, (Big Daddy Rucker), "Best Friend Blues", stuff in there about his old lady leaving with her best friend. It happens in all society, it's the oldest story in the world. But I would never consciously do anything—just from the point of humiliating myself to myself—do anything to disparage any race of people, surely not black people who have been the victims of that more than anyone else in America. I don't know what's in Leiber and Stoller's hearts and minds, I'm sure they would not *want* to do that either—but they did!'

It may be easy to conclude that to have portrayed blacks in such an unvaryingly stereotyped fashion was an error of inexorably poor taste. But that notion is less acceptable on a deeper analysis, for the material that Leiber and Stoller employed was not substantially different from that associated with blues lyrics which have constantly mirrored lower class black attitudes and traditions. It can be argued, and demonstrated, that they wrote about the environmental factors that produced the blues: the effects of drinking and gambling, working conditions in depressed areas, the pleasures and more often the disappointments of sex, migration as an escape, the constant threat of jail, etc.

Sex, food, drink, gambling are the pursuits which all blues poets have, at one time or another, described in their compositions. Are Leiber and Stoller to be blamed for working with the same material because they are not themselves black? The blues has long been considered 'devil music' by religious or middle-class blacks very largely because it emphasized the same disrespectable values which Johnny Otis was disturbed to find in those songs which Leiber and Stoller brought to his attention. Indeed the song he had in mind could so very easily have been one of a thousand or more blues and r & b songs. Take 'Wang Dang Doodle' (from the pen of black Chicago singer–composer, Willie Dixon) which refers to 'Automatic Slim', 'Razor Totin' Jim', and such characters as 'Butcher Knife Totin' Annie'. And who, for example, needs Ku Klux Klan propaganda when Otis Redding could sing 'Shout Bamalama'?

*'Lord have mercy on my soul*
*how many chickens have I stole*
*one last night, night before*
*goin' back, try to get ten, eleven more.'*

It must be accepted that there are innumerable songs of black authorship which throw a disparaging light upon the attitudes of the black race. After years spent in recording their performances for the Library of Congress, John Lomax claimed that blues singers were concerned with two things—food and sex. Paul Oliver has drawn attention to a similar phenomenon: 'If the Negro has been stereotyped it is also true that he creates his own stereotypes of himself. The Negro who acts out these stereotypes before Whites is accused of "Uncle Tomism" but in the relative privacy of the group he may still do so, unwittingly accepting the negative values that have been attributed to him. Accused of shiftlessness he can become shiftless, accused of a lack of independence he may be reluctant to accept responsibility.'[4] It is not, of course, always unwitting. Black comedians, including the now infamous Stepin Fetchit himself, have consciously paraded such negative values in front of black audiences. One of his 'in-person' albums pictures the performer in a tattered vest, trousers held up by string, and a wide-brimmed cotton-picker's hat. A flagon of hard liquor lies beside a rocking chair and titles like 'Times is Hard' or 'Police Department' are sufficient indication of his act in themselves. The Coasters were almost as well received in the r & b market as they were by a national, and therefore, largely white, audience; perhaps that strong element of lightheartedness—an approach which Leiber and Stoller shared with black comedians who 'sent themselves up'—is the least painful, least uncomfortable way of reacting to prejudice and bigotry. Perhaps, too, living up to a parody of white misconceptions represents overt aggression; it may act as a safety valve for expressions of anger, protest or violence. Paul Oliver has found similar motives in blues which are not necessarily humorous: 'The prevalence of some themes may indicate a particular function of the music, acting as a release for discharged energies which might otherwise seek more dangerous outlets.'[5]

Of course, if Leiber and Stoller had exclusively written blues for blacks as opposed to rock 'n' roll for whites, the problem of bad taste would not arise. As it is, although there were areas in which they certainly did make subtle alterations to their compositions when writing for both audiences, in all other respects they maintained the status quo. Their unique form of rock 'n' roll retained more associations with the blues than any other and, in effect, blacks were regarded in terms of a Stepin Fetchit image during twenty years of active song-writing no matter which audience their songs were aimed at. Little Willie Littlefield was poncing off the woman he lived with in 'Striking on you Baby' (Federal 12101), a Leiber and Stoller composition, as long ago as 1952. He complained that he could afford neither whisky nor wine because she failed to provide sufficient cash. Liquor is also a spur in Littlefield's 'K C Lovin''. Here the rhythm preserves the expectancy of going to Kansas City and the pleasures—'a crazy way of lovin'' or 'a bottle of Kansas City wine'—that await the singer there. As Johnny Otis has already observed, the same preoccupation with simple pleasures is to be found in Leiber and Stoller's very earliest collaborations, and on this evidence it would be wholly unjust to suggest that they made any conscious appeal to racist elements within the white audience, during the initial popularity of rock 'n' roll. By the development of having written in the same way for white, as well as black, consumption, the black man's negative values, and the myths that surround him, may have taken on an exaggerated importance as far as white listeners were concerned. Was it invariably harmful? I think not. It would, after all, be plainly absurd to suggest that Leiber and Stoller should have changed their portrayal of black people in order to prevent the continued entrenchment of a black stereotype. The sex-obsessed, gin-drinking simpleton of blues lore could not have been replaced by wholesome, clean-cut, middle-class figures such as Sidney Poitier (post-war Hollywood's guilty compensation for Stepin Fetchit?) without diluting the rebellious essence of rock 'n' roll or nullifying its all-important sense of humour.

There is, moreover, good reason to suppose that many whites are attracted to blues because it is played by blacks in the stereotype we have come to expect. That many enthusiasts cannot bear to listen to white students playing blues for blacks as opposed to rock 'n' roll for whites, the that of the performers they copy seems to indicate that blues—or for that matter, r & b or soul—is largely attractive to whites simply because it is the music of blacks. In America during the mid-fifties, and again in Britain during the r & b 'boom' of 1963/64, white teenage audiences were inclined to mythicize blacks, copying more than their music. Styles of dress were also adopted and Negro slang was appropriated; on coming to live in London in 1963 I recollect ascribing the generic term 'Solomons' to the city's West Indian population out of a devotion to Solomon Burke whom I was particularly predisposed to worship. Today, teenagers in the North of England cannot enjoy soul without, it seems, appearing to be as 'cool and sharp' as those who sing it. It is a phenomenon that cannot have escaped Leiber and Stoller; when The Coasters records began to transcend r & b sales, they revealed a greater emphasis on such idiosyncracies of black culture as dress, speech or bearing than in their earlier records. Far from pandering to racialist elements, the emphasis actually seemed attractive to white adolescents who felt a need to romanticize or emulate the black ghetto life-style with which The Coasters were readily identified.

* * *

A black life-style is far from being the only aspect of the blues to have remained in Leiber and Stoller's compositions throughout the fifties and sixties. 'Kansas City' is a blues of migration essentially no different to 'Keep on Rollin' which, more than any other Coasters recording, illustrates the tenacity of particular blues images. One stanza:

*'Got my cash in a matchbox, my clothes in a brown paper hold*

*I'm gonna keep on rollin' as far as I can go.'*

harks back to Blind Lemon Jefferson's 'Matchbox Blues':

*'Sittin' here wonderin' will a matchbox hold my clothes*
*I ain't got so many matches but I got so far to go.'*

Some of the 'poetry' performed by The Coasters was borrowed from a common stock as old or older than the beginning of recorded blues. 'Dimples' are usually in the jaw (Willie Mabon's 'I don't Know', Blind Lemon's 'Booger Rooger Blues', John Lee Hooker's blues of that title) but it would be surprising if 'Dimples in your Knees' from 'Down Home Girl' is without similar precedents. 'For you pretty baby I break my Momma's rule' and 'I really love your peaches, gonna shake your tree', from the Ertegun–Lewis composition 'Lovey Dovey', are particularly familiar.

Vividness of expression, often witty or humorous, is one of the blues' most exciting characteristics; Jerry Leiber was particularly adept at condensing an amusing, succinct expression within a single line:

'*Sometimes my stomach think somebody done broke my neck*' (Hungry)
'*You're gonna need an ocean of calamine lotion*' (Poison Ivy)
'*She can stretch a greenback dollar bill from here to Kingdom come*' (She Can)
'*That horse took off like a Man O' War*' (Stewball)
'*My heart's like this freight train full of fire and smoke*' (Keep on Rollin')

Phrases like these can be extracted as little gems. Whether metaphorical, similial, witty, poetic, or a combination of each, they conjure up poignant, powerful or startling images by virtue of their sheer economy. In The Coasters rock 'n' roll songs they recall the artistry of such blues poets as B. B. King ('laid in the ghetto flats cold and numb, I heard the rats tell the bedbugs to give the roaches some') or Guitar Nubbitt ('I whistled to my shotgun and it crawled down off the wall'). Some again will not be unfamiliar to country blues admirers; 'Keep on Rollin' runs the gamut of freight train and railroad allusions to be found in rural blues, and 'M and O blues' (Walter Davis) and 'My Baby got a Heart like a Piece of Railroad Steel' (Charlie Patton), are lyrically similar.

It has been said that most blues are dramatic monologues, dramatic because people are talking together, a monologue because only one person is usually heard to speak in the song. On this basis (which contradicts the widely accepted conception of blues as a solitary and introspective lyricism) Jerry Leiber and Mike Stoller are superb playwrights while The Coasters are actors of a rare excellence. 'It was Leiber and Stoller,' said Nat Hentoff, 'who made several of their songs into compact plays in which there were definite lines and rhythmic motifs for particular voices. I am not saying that Leiber and Stoller have become the Brechts of rhythm and blues, but they have approached their work with a freshness, intelligence, and humour that are terribly rare among writers for the pop market.'[6] While Hentoff hesitates to compare them with Brecht, John Dunton thought Shakespeare was more appropriate:

*'Take the blood out of an alligator, take the left eye out*
*of a fish,*
*Take the skin off a frog and mix it all up in a dish,*
*Add a cup of green swamp water and then count from one*
*to nine*
*Spit it over your left shoulder you got Alligator Wine.'*

Commenting on this verse from 'Alligator Wine' (OKeh 7101) a song written by Leiber and Stoller for Screamin' Jay Hawkins in 1957, Dunton queries, 'Who can deny its impact, and the insane logic that puts it on a par with one of the most famous potions in English literature?'[7] namely the witch's brew from Shakespeare's *Macbeth*.

By now it will have become apparent that Leiber and Stoller (for the latter too was concerned with making the phraseology accurately idiomatic) employed enormous use of dramatic monologues and dialogues. In 'Riot in Cell Block No. 9' there is a line for the warden and the prisoner, Scarface Jones. A policeman, stool-pigeon, prosecuting attorney, and judge all have something to say in 'Framed'. The Coasters are for ever thinking aloud, conferring among themselves and addressing others. There are conversations between the lead or bass and a dance-hall pick-up ('I must be Dreaming'); a cafe proprietor ('Smokey Joe's Cafe', 'Down in Mexico'); the father of 'Young Blood'; assorted girl-friends ('Hungry', 'One kiss led to Another') and even no one in particular:

*'Well somebody slapped me on the back,*
*said "Stewball loves a muddy track".'*

Snatches of conversation filter out of a television programme in 'Along came Jones'; 'Three Cool Cats' verbalize their lust for three cool chicks, and an instruction to an elevator girl to lead to the dry goods floor precedes a complicated discussion between client and salesman in 'Shoppin' for Clothes'. Even inarticulate objects and creatures are blessed with the ability to speak. 'Hold on Jim, give me time to think' pleads the 'Idol with The Golden Head'. 'Gimme your car-keys and gimme your watch, give 'em to me or I'll shoot' threatens a monkey in 'Run Red Run' while the insects in 'Bull Tick Waltz' include a green hornet who boasts:

*'Where's the dance floor? I just gotta get on it*
*You ain't seen nuthin' 'til you seen me doggone it.'*

When they wrote for The Coasters other writers including Dallas Frazier ('Ridin' Hood'), Doc Pomus, and Mort Shuman ('Snake and The Bookworm'), Bobby Darin ('Wait a Minute'), Lewis ('Bad Detective'), and Lover Patterson ('Tain't nothin' to Me') employed an identical technique. The songs they contributed contain, without exception, asides, commands, or spoken interjections of various kinds. As late as 1965, when he composed The Coasters' soul number, 'Crazy Baby', Billy Guy could not resist following suit:

*'I need a love and need it bad so come on over and share*
*my pad,*
*She said, "I'm not jokin', my heart's wide open."'*

The blues is riddled with an idiomatic language which has long intrigued those who might call themselves ethnomusicologists. I need quote no more than a couple of 'household' blue lines (for example, 'She said, "You gotta boy-child comin' he's gonna be a son of a gun,"' or 'I said, "Good morning blues, give me your right hand"') to show that the insertion of fragmentary vernacular is inextricably weaved into blues composition. Jive expressions had a double-edged function, strengthening the identity of blacks as a separate group while alienating whites for whom the argot was mysterious if not indecipherable. The language of rock 'n' roll functioned in the same way; as an in-group terminology for teenagers which succeeded in alienating white adults. Nervous Norvous (Jimmy Drake) was one of those to enjoy a couple of novelty records which capitalized on adolescent colloquialism although, in comparison with those made by Leiber and Stoller, his records give today's listener an unusual experience of limited appeal. Jerry Leiber wrote in a far more durable mixture of normally idiomatic speech and attractive, amusing expressions derived originally from Negro slang. 'Hip', according to one old dictionary, originally meant 'melancholia, the blues'. The Coasters were a decidedly hip bunch of cats: they swore by the pretty Lord, motivated groovy, dug the scenes, done lost their cool, flipped their lids, blew their stacks, caught the lovin' bug and hung out in way-out pads with their crazy chicks, mommas, boppers, babies, kittens, or spodee-os. Everything was a knockout except squares and they were a doggone drag. Most of this rock 'n' roll glossary has now passed into common usage. Between fifteen and twenty years ago it was obscure, possibly even dangerous to white adults who reacted with predictable fear. Andrew Weiner has recalled 'a fairly strong element of paranoia in even supposedly good-natured and humorous attacks on the new music. A popular satirical record of the time (by the aforementioned Buchanan and Goodman) linked the rock 'n' roll craze with a second and apparently equally bizarre paranoia-inducing fad, flying saucers.'[8]

At the same time, rhythm and blues was not for The Coasters a personal expression of the singer's *immediate* experience. As we have seen, Jerry Leiber was a dramatist with a distinct detachment from the problems and emotions to which his fictional characters related. When Billy Guy sang of employment as a garbage collector in his own song 'Wake Me, Shake Me', it was not a personal recollection but a dramatic comedy. How often this can be said of all blues singers is debatable; where The Coasters are concerned there is no room for argument. Nor does it invalidate their work in any sense, for it adds two extra dimensions. The composer must employ an unusually developed imagination, while the singers need to invest their performances with a particular authority and dramatic skill. 'The Coasters,' Leiber has said, 'were almost like a group of vaudeville actors. All of them, in some way or another, were comedians.'[9] Billy Guy, in particular, was a superb mimic. An articulate, family man, he is given to sprinkling phrases like *'per se' and 'pro rata'* during his conversation, but not to slapping his thighs or rolling his eyes. Yet for ten years he portrayed a variety of wholly believable mindless, lecherous, indolent hoodlums. 'Guy,' commented Stoller, 'was really extraordinarily clever. He had a great sense of timing. Most of the others more or less took direction from us but he would often have a great deal to do with the way a line was finally presented. Guy had a kind of rapport, I don't know how to express it exactly, but through the characters he played it was a kind of a slap back at Uncle Tomism. He had a very keen sense of humour and it certainly wasn't Tomming for the white audience. He—in fact none of the group—took exception to the situations they were placed in. There were times when they creased up. After all, they were funny and I think they experienced them as being funny and that was it.'

The Coasters records are indisputably funny, a factor which, in itself, sets them apart from other 'conventional' rock 'n' roll performers. To sustain a series of successful records in which humour was such a vital ingredient says much for the creativity and imagination of Leiber's lyrics; they very often reveal a social awareness unparalleled in rock 'n' roll. It was a unique form of comedy, a cross of entertaining minstrel show patter with the kind of joke that all isolated or depressed groups of people tell against themselves. It mixes not only the humour that is used by lower-class blacks to alleviate feelings of misery and distress but also the humour which is employed to express animosity and disrespect for the structure of white society. For Mike Stoller it was 'an attempt to satirize all society, not just white society. The black community was, after all, hanging by the financial power-strings of the white society. Black society was created by the white power structure and we satirized both—all of the songs had this element.' Economically, socially, culturally—the White Anglo-Saxon Protestant has dominated the U.S.A. in every way; it is unnecessary to provide examples: However, since 1955, the styles and creeds of traditional Americanism have become increasingly irrelevant. Rock 'n' roll helped to undermine this homogeneity because it was a vehicle in which minority racial groups—blacks, Jewish immigrants, Puerto Ricans, Mexican–Americans, even the 'poor white trash' of the South—and young people as a whole, were able to repudiate almost everything the Great American Dream stood for. At the broad end of this spectrum, The Coasters were simply irreverent to those canons which White America held in high esteem. Conformity, authority, tradition, a sense of duty towards one's parents, the piety of the honest, the hard work ethic, the dutiful suppression of dissonant pleasures—all these were questioned with a ready boldness and subversive wit that went largely unnoticed at the time. Perhaps it was deliberately ignored, for the impiety of Leiber and Stoller (by origin, Jewish) and the group (all Negroes invariably born in The South) had a tinge of blasphemy about it. Blacks, immigrants or their descendants were expected to show gratitude towards the system; they were not supposed to stand up and criticize it. Leiber and Stoller, however, did, and today this can be recognized in their every song.

In particular, police methods of arrest on suspicion ('I was walkin' down the street mindin' my own affairs, when two policemen grabbed me er—unawares') and the notorious nature of the Southern judiciary ('when the judge came down, poured whisky on my head, turned around to the jury, an' said "convict this man, he is drunk", what could I do?') are satirized mercilessly. Intolerance of any kind (a Buddhist, an African, assorted freaks, an FBI agent, a poet, and a couple of Russian students all share the communal 'Soul Pad'), and the hypocrisy of fidelity ('Everybody's Woman looks better to me than mine') receive the same fate. Managerial power ('My boss is a big fat slob') takes a hammering, a theme which is also implicit in the gulf between rich and poor. The gap between generations comes over as a poor second in comparison with the gap between blacks and the nation's actual—as well as symbolic—boss-man. Take, for example, 'What about Me', a song which Leiber and Stoller originally wrote for blues-singer Larry Evans (Fabor 4009) around 1956. The Coasters revived it in 1959:

'*He's got a house made of glass, got his own swimming pool,* (*what a gas*)
*We got a one-room shack, a pile of sticks by the railroad track.*

*Well, what about us, what about us,*
*Don't wanna cause no fuss but what about us.*

*He's with a beautiful chick every night of the week,* (*pretty slick*)
*We're too poor hung-up souls, girls won't touch with ten-foot poles.*

*He goes to eat at The Ritz, big steaks* (*that's the breaks*)
*We eat a harmony grits from a bag* (*what a drag*).

*He's gotta car made of suede with a black leather top* (*got it made*)
*If we go out on dates we go in a box on a roller skates.*'

There were many other targets. Self-consciousness and male chauvinism are made to appear faintly ridiculous in 'Three Cool Cats'. The wicked innuendo apparent in that song's situation, and the observations of the principal characters, made it necessary for it to appear as the B side of 'Charlie Brown'.

'*Three cool cats* x 2
*parked on the corner in a beat-up car*
*dividing up a nickel candy bar*
*talkin' all about how sharp they are*
*These three cool cats.*

*Three cool chicks* x 2
*Walkin' down the street a swingin' their hips*
*splitting up a bag of potato chips*
*and three cool cats did three big flips*
*for three cool chicks.*

*Up popped the first cool cat,*
*He said, "Man look at that, man do you see what I see?"*
*"I want that middle chick!"—"I want that little chick!"*
*"Hey man, save one chick for me!"*

*Three cool chicks* x 2
*They look like angels from up above*
*an' three cool cats really fell in love*
*but three cool chicks made real fools of—*
*these three cool cats.'*

'Three Cool Cats' has a moral for everyone who thought he was living dangerously by propping up The Odeon on a Saturday afternoon. Finally, even the puerility of television programmes was pointed up in 'Along Came Jones'. On this occasion, Jerry Leiber's ability to write witty lines ultimately lessens the force of his intentions; his lyrics are so much funnier than any TV western dialogue we've ever heard.

*'I flopped down in my easy chair and turned on channel two*
*a bad gunslinger named Salty Sam was chasin' poor sweet Sue*
*he trapped her in the old saw-mill an' said with an evil laugh*
*"If you don't gimme the deed to your ranch I'll saw you all in half"*
*An' then he grabbed her* (*an' then*) *he tied her up* (*an' then*)
*he turned on the buzz-saw* (*an' then, an' then*)

*Heh, heh, an' then Along Came Jones**
*Tall thin Jones*
*Slow walking Jones, slow talkin' Jones,*
*Along came lonely lanky Jones.*

*Commercial came on so I got up to get myself a snack*
*you shoulda seen what was on that screen by the time that I got back*
*down in the old abandoned mine sweet Sue was a havin' fits*
*that villain said, "Gimme the key to your ranch or I'll blow you all to bits"*
*An' then he grabbed her (an' then) he tied her up (an' then)*
*he lit the fuse to the dynamite (an' then, an' then)*

*I got so bugged I turned it off an' turned on another show*
*but there was the same old shoot-em-up an' the same old rodeo*
*Salty Sam was a tryin' to stuff Sweet Sue in a burlap sack*
*He said, "If you don't give me the deed to your ranch I'm gonna throw you on the railroad track"*
*An' then he grabbed her . . .'*

* Repeat

*  *  *

Apart from the strongly developed satirical thread which connects virtually all of their songs, the most important difference between blues and Leiber and Stoller's brand of rock 'n' roll lay in the way in which The Coasters records were produced. Structurally, they continued to use the commonest features of blues composition—the twelve bar form and the three-line stanza—when writing rock 'n' roll. Mike Stoller recalls his first meeting with Jerry Leiber: 'He showed me the lyrics he had written in his school-book. I could see from the ditto-marks under the first lines of most verses that a lot of them were blues!' In this sphere, there was very little change. From most of Littlefield's repertoire to The Robins' 'Hatchet Man' and up to 'I'm a Hog for you Baby' and 'Keep on Rollin'' for The Coasters, the traditional three-line blues stanza was reserved for less elaborate ideas. Occasionally, two lines, as in 'Charlie Brown', would suffice. Admittedly, it was not always possible to relate a complicated story in verses of three lines each and, as plots became more complex, other stanzas, usually four lines but sometimes five ('Dance') or six ('Bull Tick Waltz'), were employed. More startling was Leiber and Stoller's practice of breaking up the verse patterns into all manner of ingenious shapes so as to provide each of the quartet—particularly the bass singer—and the saxophonist with something to say. Commented Mike Stoller: 'Jerry has always been involved in theatre and we discovered that as each song was being written, even before we rehearsed them with the group, the lines seemed to call for assignment. We had always been very much taken with a bass voice—even on our early things we might have had a deep musical "dow-ooop" effect—and we found ourselves with a tremendous bass singer with a fantastic timbre in Dub Jones.'

Jones was rarely under-employed. Take, for example, 'Wake me, Shake me'. Coldly annotated on paper, it is difficult to imagine a more contrived arrangement:

'*Why don't you* (slow bass-prominent harmony), *wake me,* (faster-in-unison)
*yeah* (bass) *shake me,* (unison) *yeah* (bass)
*Don't let me sleep too late* (unison)
*Oh* (lead tenor) *gotta get up in the morning about a quarter to eight* (unison)

Both lyrics and melody were lifted from an old spiritual,

'Swing Low Sweet Chariot' or, as The Staple Singers called it, 'Let Me Ride' (Veejay 846):

*'Why don't you wake me, shake me, don't let me sleep too late,*
*We'll get to heaven in the morning, swing on the golden gate*
*Don't you know I'm bound for higher ground*
*I'm singing the glory sound.'*

Billy Guy, who is given the writer's credit, had simply substituted garbage trucks for chariots. Compare the refrain of 'Let Me Ride' with Billy Guy's secularized solo verse:

*'Look over yonder, what did I see*
*two black chariots Lord coming after me*
*two white horses running side by side*
*swing down sweet chariot Lord and let this child ride.'*
*('Let me Ride')*

*'I said look over yonder a what did I see*
*I see two big garbage trucks a comin' after me*
*a pickin' up cans I said side by side*
*why don't you swing down sweet garbage truck and let your buddy ride.'*
('Wake me, Shake me')

Despite the obvious lyrical similarity to 'Swing Low Sweet Chariot', no gospel music was ever so complicated as 'Wake me, Shake me'.

Tenor saxophone phrases from King Curtis replace bass 'yeahs' in the refrain when it is repeated for a third and fourth time. In addition, I use the word 'unison' loosely. Where the casual listener might hear no more than a quartet singing the same words together, Mike Stoller hears a simultaneous combination of melodies and would prefer the term 'two part invention', a name given originally by

Johann Sebastian Bach to describe a type of short keyboard work in two part counterpoint. It was entirely unprecedented to produce a black vocal group in this lavish, extraordinarily attentive, fashion.

Jerry Wexler: 'Most of the producers, such as Hy Weiss, Leo Rogers, and Morty Craft, would line up their groups in droves in the control room and push them up to the microphones where they would sing their songs in one take. Not only were there no arrangements, but the band (standard four rhythm and one tenor saxophone) would, in all likelihood, not have heard of the song being cut, and would rarely even know in what key to begin playing. As soon as one group finished two sides, another would be escorted forward on the assembly line.'[10] These unscrupulous methods very often produced an undisciplined but engaging kind of quadruple counterpoint, each man humming, sighing, burping, and droning away, a law unto himself. Atlantic was one of the very few companies prepared to invest time and money in rehearsing black groups. But while their vocals are in tune and their arrangements tightly polished, groups like The Clovers, The Drifters, or The Cardinals still remained faithful to a traditional adaptation of a 'barbershop' style of singing where a tenor, baritone, and bass would accompany the lead, usually another tenor. The Robins had frequently followed this pattern—The Coasters almost never.

'The Coasters,' wrote Jim Delehant, 'were a radically different group for Atlantic, a real change from The Clovers or The Drifters, who depended solely on interpreting blues material. The Coasters were the creation of Jerry Leiber and Mike Stoller, probably the first image-makers in the business. Leiber and Stoller wrote music specifically for each member of the group and taught each how to sing his part. Then they went into the studio and moulded a perfect record by explaining to the engineer exactly what they wanted. Even on a scratchy 78, The Coasters sound comes through just as crisp as a modern Beatles or Beach Boys record. Just compare "Steamboat" (1955) by The Drifters to "Down in Mexico" (1956) by The Coasters. They are both beautiful records, but The Coasters is much more modern anyway you look at it—concept, harmony, instrumentation, clarity of sound.'[11] While Leiber and Stoller knew the sound they were after, Tom Dowd, Atlantic's chief engineer and a pioneer in recording techniques, experimented until they were more than satisfied:

'Tommy Dowd knew so many ways in which to try and accommodate what we wanted, he's a fantastically inventive man. We all spent a lot of time on the 8-track machine going over many takes, again and again, until we got the perfect reading. But even back on "Riot in Cell Block No. 9" we had chopped the tapes about. On that record, I think the refrain is the same one all the way through the song. We took the refrain we liked best, duplicated it, and shoved it back again. There were occasional gimmick effects but that wasn't really a big part of our work. Rather we would sometimes slow a track down because it would feel better, sometimes we'd speed it up because the words came out seemingly more enunciated. Long before most studios had a VFO, (variable frequency oscillator) which can change the speed of things as it turned, we had speeded a wrap. On the spindle that the tape runs against we could take a piece of editing tape and wind it around the capstan. One wrap would tend to change the speed and if you wrapped it twice it would speed it that much more. I think we may have done that first with Bunny Robyn in LA.'

The human voice—for many years the only noticeable part of a black group record and, traditionally, its most important contribution—was no longer a sacred entity. Much to the chagrin of 'purist' vocal group collectors, it could be moulded, distorted, electronically tampered with, almost computed. A bass voice could be slowed down to ensure that it came across with just the right touch of indolence while natural flaws could be ironed out, perhaps by cutting the tape to remove consonants like 'S' from the ends of words and sticking the bits together again. Leiber and Stoller could, on occasion, be disrespectful towards the idiom in which they worked. Who could deny the artificiality of speeding up the tape for novel effect as occurred, for example, in 'Little Egypt' or 'Charlie Brown'? It adds nothing to the performance except to remind one, somewhat uncomfortably, of Ross Bagdasarian's work with The Chipmunks, The Nutty Squirrels, and similar nursery delights. Leiber and Stoller conceived and created the most brilliant, dynamic, and ingenious of all pre-1960 records: but, ultimately, they were responsible for ushering out the spontaneous simplicity of an era that will never return and—in paying tributes of this kind—one should not forget those who would claim that imaginative production has no place in blues or authentic rock 'n' roll.

As black group records became increasingly complex white rock 'n' rollers were curiously slow to jump on the plagiarist band-wagon. Infrequently, moronic bass voices would appear out of nowhere—'No dice son you gotta work late', from Eddie Cochran's 'Summertime Blues' (Liberty 55144) is even more familiar than 'You better leave my daughter alone' or 'Eat up all your beans and boy then clear right on out'—and, on rare occasions, one or two white performers went further. The Pacers, a group from Arkansas, included a reference to a number of mythical Western gunslingers—as well as the 'Searchin' ' alley piano figure—for their record 'Texas Lil' (Razorback 133). Gene Simmons, a rockabilly from Tupelo, Mississippi, borrowed the entire Leiber/Stoller/Coasters sound, including a positively stunning facsimile of King Curtis, in order to provide 'Charlie Brown' with an equally juvenile relation, 'Bad Boy Willie' (Checker 948):

*'Wella way down South where they play it cool*
*Bad Boy Willie is the talk of the school.*
*The teacher call the roll when the clock strikes eight*
(bass voice) *Here come Willie—he's late.*

*Wella rubber bands and paper was a Willie's delight,*
*an' little girls with pigtails he ties 'em tight*
*The teacher turned around as the chalk hit the floor*
(bass voice) *Please, please Teacher, I won't do it no more.'*

None of these white artists repeated such ideas on their subsequent records. Nor, with such rare exceptions, were they at all anxious to exploit lyrical situations which had proved to be so popular for The Coasters. Revivals of The Coasters' songs (The Hollies' re-working of the nursery rhyme-based 'Ain't That Just Like Me'; Tom Rush's 'My Baby comes to Me' and 'I'm a Hog for you Baby' from Screaming Lord Sutch) usually chose to resuscitate from, among all their recordings, those with a broadly universal theme or application. Urban blues satire was a guaranteed form of immunization from the white cover records which plagued almost every other major black group or performer throughout the nineteen-fifties. There was, however, one not insignificant attempt; a British actor, Bernard Bresslaw—famed for playing type-cast characters for whom the word 'gormless' was invented—did cover 'Charlie Brown'.

Ultimately, if the manner in which Leiber and Stoller gave individual lines to each member of the group was extremely distinctive, it also tended to confirm the mass-media impression that blacks were unable to open their mouths without making a wheedling, threatening, or simply dim remark. Stick a pin in any one of the group and he will oblige with an exclamation in a deep and funny voice. Had four white boys performed the same material, parodying the black man's speech in the same necessarily indelicate fashion, they would not have been heard outside of juke-boxes in the white-owned honky-tonks of Alabama and Mississippi. As it was, 'Texas Lil' and 'Bad Boy Willie' never sold a light.

CHAPTER FIVE

# SHOPPIN' FOR HITS

THE world-wide popularity of 'Yakety Yak' and 'Charlie Brown' guaranteed The Coasters a permanent shrine in rock 'n' roll's Hall of Fame. Had they never entered a recording studio again they would have remained an institution on the strength of these two enormous hits. Any other vocal group would have followed a couple of timeless classics with a slew of records whose artistic qualities gradually diminished. The Coasters made a number of subsequent records at least as good as 'Yakety Yak' including three, 'Poison Ivy', 'Shoppin' for Clothes', and 'Little Egypt', which brought vocal group production to increasingly dazzling new heights.

If *Billboard*'s r & b chart is an accurate guide, 'Poison Ivy' was The Coasters' most popular record among black audiences, topping the list on two occasions and remaining in the top ten for over three months towards the end of 1959. Quite unlike their usual situation comedies, the song had no specifically black nor remotely philosophical application. A simple but delightful play on words, 'Poison Ivy' defies pretentious analysis; as Mike Stoller would say 'it was funny and that was that'. And sure enough, while the absence of any satirical flavour was atypical of Jerry Leiber's work the comic possibilities of the pun—you don't have to be a botanist to get the joke—were explored in the succinct but rich and candid vernacular endemic of all his lyrics:

*'She's pretty as a daisy but look out man she's crazy*
*she'll really do you in if you let her get under your skin.'*

Few records around in 1959 were as instantly catchy as this. As contagious as the diseases to which the group refer ('measles make you bumpy and mumps'll make you lumpy'), the melody was accentuated by the guitarist whose memorable introductory riff is repeated throughout the song. Yes—the tune's good too. It's another of the fundamental reasons for the group's appeal. If you *did* miss the point you could still enjoy the sound. The flip-side, 'I'm a Hog for you', got through to a lot of customers as well:

*'One little piggy ate a pizza*
*one piggy ate potato chips*
*but this little piggy's comin' over your house*
*he's gonna nip a load of your sweet lips.'*

The words were bound to raise a chuckle but the instrumental break must have raised a few eyebrows. Ultimately, it's the finest on any Coasters' disc. The guitarist, probably Mickey Baker, plays one shrill note for nigh on thirty seconds—he picks at the same string relentlessly, forty-five times. Beneath him a baritone sax grunts and a tenor sax squeals—grunt, snort, squeal, grunt, snort, squeal; it sounds like fifty horns at once but it's just King Curtis spliced up and stuck together again to create an utterly stupendous aural picture of feeding time down at the trough.

The use of session men like Barney Kessel and Mickey Baker overshadowed The Coasters' regular guitarist, Adolph Jacobs who, in December 1959, left to be replaced by Sonny Forriest, a jazz-inflected picker from Pendleton, North Carolina. Forriest learned to play the guitar while stationed in England in the U.S.A.F. and, prior to joining The Coasters, he had worked with Sil Austin, Dee Clark, and Big Jay McNeely. According to Atlantic's files, his debut with the group, in February 1960, was a massive session—five tracks instead of the usual one or two. Of these, 'Besame Mucho' was so orthodox as to be unusual. Part one, virtually an instrumental by King Curtis, was marginally more exciting than Part two, a solo by Dub Jones with minimal support from the rest of the group. But both were pretty dull while 'Snake and The Bookworm' wasn't much better. The only Doc Pomus–Mort Shuman composition which The Coasters recorded, it was more notable for a piano solo by Mike Stoller. The duo's songs of adolescent passion ('A Teenager in Love', 'My Private Joy', 'Save The Last Dance for Me', 'Angel of Love', 'So Close to Heaven' etc.) were of a kind The Coasters regularly ignored and although 'Snake and The Bookworm' was an attempt at sly humour it came across as the sort of song Leiber and Stoller might have composed in one of their couldn't care less moods. That left Billy Guy's complex, gospel rip-off 'Wake me Shake me' and one sadly neglected goodie, 'Lady-like', about a butch young girl who wears a black leather jacket and rides a 'motor sickle'. She's the counterpart to the hero of Leiber and Stoller's 1955 hit, 'Black Denim Trousers and Motor cycle Boots'. He roared up and down with an eagle on his back, axle grease in his hair, and a tattoo on his arm with picture of a heart, saying 'Mother I love You'. The heroine of 'Lady-like' walks like a sailor, wears tattoos to disguise her acne and comes in for a lot of criticism the tone of which is both generational and gently moralistic. It ain't lady-like to ride a motor bike, hang around the blue-light diner or goof on the corner with the neighbourhood rat-pack. 'Take off them ole beatnik clothes,' sings Dub Jones in his role of parental admonitor. It could have been a real jewel but the setting wasn't quite up to par—and yet compared to what immediately followed, it was nothing less than brilliant.

In June 1960 The Coasters spent two days recording an album of twelve standard tunes written by Tin Pan Alley's most celebrated composers including Jerome Kern, Johnny Mercer, and Cole Porter. While Atlantic may have wanted to break the group into the supper club circuit, the idea seems to have been mooted by Carl Gardner: 'Leiber and Stoller knew that we were versatile and able to sing all kinds of tunes and I had steadily kept after them to do some pop songs. I had always wanted to do things like 'Moonlight in Vermont' with strings and eventually I got the opportunity. It was a very quick session costing around 7,000 dollars. Leiber and Stoller put the orchestrations on tape and we went into the studios and overdubbed our voices. It was done so swiftly I didn't get a chance to really go and study how I wanted to do those tunes.' The album sported an uncharacteristically snobbish sleeve-note from *Billboard*'s Music Editor, Paul Ackerman: 'It taps an even broader vein of the consumer market than earlier records of The Coasters. It will appeal not only to youthful fans but to adults of cultivated and more advanced musical taste.' This philistine played it once on first purchase and again for the purpose of this book. The appeal on both occasions is hard to explain but the shudders outweighed any frisson of joy. Carl Gardner had four tunes, Gunter and Jones took three each while Billy Guy, who sang very much like he always had, was permitted just two. His voice can scarcely have been more out of place and he sounds distinctly uncomfortable. Ackerman describes his performance as 'flavourful' although he may well have been referring to the bubble-gum which Guy had evidently forgotten to remove from his cheek. Everyone else seems to enjoy themselves. Dub Jones does a passable imitation of Jimmy Ricks, Gunter is plainly glad to get a look in and Carl Gardner, who sings with obvious relish, is very probably doing what he loves most of all. As to the reaction of Coasters' fans, posterity is silent. I don't suppose anyone shouted 'sell-out'. It was taken for granted that sooner or later, rock 'n' rollers would be compelled to sing what had passed for 'adult' music and, like Carl, most were only too pleased to prove their versatility.

Fortunately, all concerned redeemed themselves on the very next session. In July 1960, The Coasters and Leiber and Stoller trooped into Atlantic's funky old studio and emerged with 'Shoppin for Clothes'. 'This,' said Jerry Wexler, 'was a masterpiece in every respect.'[1] 'I think,' recalled Leiber, 'I probably liked "Shoppin' for Clothes" best of all.'[2] In many ways it was a truly remarkable record. To begin with it was not—as at first supposed—written by Leiber and Stoller. To appreciate the full story of 'Shoppin' for Clothes' we need to go back to Los Angeles where, in 1956, bluesman Kent Harris recorded two of his own compositions, 'Clothesline' and 'Cops and Robbers' (Crest 1030), under the pseudonym of 'Boogaloo'. Born in Oklahoma City in 1930, Harris had travelled to L.A. in 1952 and obtained a songwriting contract with Sylvester Cross who owned Crest, a small local company which specialized in rockabilly. Harris's first record, 'Big Fat Lie' c & w 'Talk about a Party' (Crest 1014) was issued as by Boogaloo and his Gallant Crew, a name which disguised a couple of Louis Jordan flavoured blues of little distinction. By paring down the instruments to a piano, guitar, and drums, Harris achieved a tight blues unit comparable to the sound behind Chuck Berry on, for example, 'No Money Down' (Chess 1615). It is more than probable that Berry's witty and thoroughly obsessive love of automobile gadgetry inspired Harris enough to extend those same qualities to a song about—not cars—but clothes. Following closely on Berry's clipped, half-spoken, half-sung Chicago blues format, he composed 'Clothesline'. Published by the Cross-owned American Music, it is probably the funniest blues ever committed to wax. 'Clothesline' was not a monstrous seller and nothing more was heard of Kent Harris or his astonishing song until four years later when The Coasters recorded it under the fresh title of 'Shoppin' for Clothes'. The writers' credit was given as 'Elmo Glick', a mysterious cognomen which Leiber and Stoller had already used on The Drifters 'Dance with Me' (Atlantic 2040) and many occasions since. The words of 'Shoppin' for Clothes' were not unlike those for 'Clothesline', but I am unable to quote from either composition in order to illustrate the point. Permission to do so was refused by the Aberbach Group of Music Publishing

Companies who, in a letter dated 20 November 1973, told me that, over a great many years, that firm had had a very amicable relationship with Jerry Leiber and Mike Stoller and for that reason they were very reluctant to grant any permissions which might possibly in any way have constituted an embarrassment to them. They said that while they did not believe that these songs would have constituted such an embarrassment, they felt that the potential was sufficient and denied my request with reluctance. They felt sure that this would not create any hardship for me in pursuing my work since, in their view, the material was of no great importance in relation to Messrs. Leiber and Stoller and accordingly they suggested that I proceeded along different lines.

Jerry Leiber himself might agree that 'Shoppin' for Clothes' was too important a record to be ignored altogether. While he did not write it, he subsequently claimed that no deception was intended: 'I heard that song on an obscure label and the idea ... uh ... killed me but it was unrealized. It had two good lines in it but there was—you know—someone just didn't finish it, didn't really write it and sometime, I don't remember when, I told Mike about it and we tried to contact the record company which was defunct, and we tried to contact the writer and we couldn't and so I just took it upon myself to write it and we recorded it and it was always a favourite inside the house. It never sold two records but we always loved it because it was a definitive piece on that whole scene. I mean it covers a multitude of sin ...'[3]

Allowing for the fact that Leiber was in the process of collecting his thoughts as he spoke, his explanation begs a few questions. Crest, the record company to which he referred was still having hits in 1961 (e.g. Glen Campbell's 'Turn Around Look at Me') and cannot have been quite as obscure as he thought. Moreover, his recollection of Harris' composition—unrealized, unfinished—is distinctly uncharitable. There were more 'good lines' in it than there were in

'Shoppin' for Clothes'. In all probability, he had forgotten some of Harris' wittiest couplets and misinterpreted the occasional expression. But to get a joke it is usually necessary to understand the words and 'Shoppin' for Clothes' was, in some respects, a deliberate departure from 'Clothesline'. While funny in itself, the lightning speed with which Harris ripped through his ghetto patois only helped to nullify the impact of the lyric. His record may have been easily understood by the largely black audience at which it was aimed but a straightforward and concise statement was necessary to entice white listeners. Leiber and Stoller truncated the lyric, halved the tempo and ensured that everyone could understand the words without straining. Whatever the ethics involved, they created a work of consummative virtuosity.

The song was now a play with two parts—Billy Guy as a client and Dub Jones as salesman—while Gardner and Gunter hum softly between the principal characters' conversation like some ineffable Greek chorus. Jones describes all the ridiculous accessories, the solid gold buttons, the camel-hair collar, even—and this is the killer—the cutaway flapover twice, so plausibly you have to believe in them all. Even the sartorially unconscious would find his manner hopelessly seductive. Before the record ends you want that suit as much as Billy Guy and when he's refused credit, his dreadful anguish is shared by the listener. Both he and Jones gave the most sensitive performances of their recording careers while the accompaniment was stark, daring, and perfectly sympathetic. King Curtis and the drummer, Gary Chester, crown this exquisite recording with a rapport one can only marvel at.

In a record that was so full of wondrous moments, the fact that the session guitarist was none other than Phil Spector should not pass unmentioned. In 1959 he had recorded for 3-Trey, an Atlantic distributed label owned by Lee Hazlewood and Lester Sill who subsequently sent him to New York where he served an apprenticeship with Leiber and Stoller. Spector supervised Atlantic sessions by The

Johnny Otis
*Inset:* (Top to bottom) Herman Lubinksy, Bill Cook, Little Esther.

*Top left:* The Flairs. Left to right: Cornel Gunter, George Hollis, Kenneth Byley, Thomas Miller.
*Top right:* The Robins. *Photo: Norbert Hess*
*Bottom:* The Johnny Otis Band 1950. *Photo: Norbert Hess*

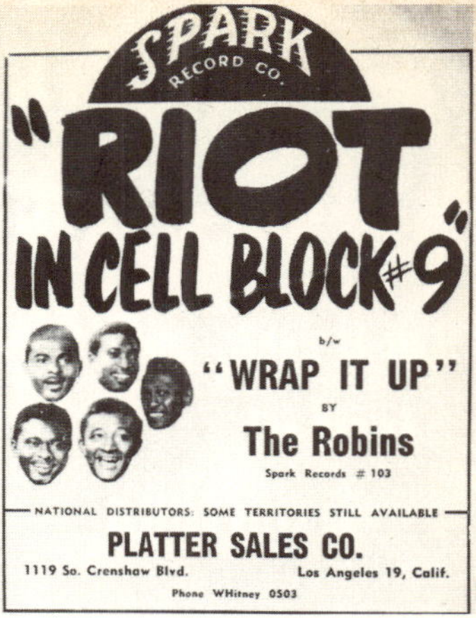

*Top left:* The Robins. *Photo: Norbert Hess*
*Top right:* Cashbox Advert 1954. *Photo: Dick Horlick/Norbert Hess*
*Bottom:* Grady Chapman. *Photo: Norbert Hess*

*Left:* The Cadets.
*Above:* Bobby Nunn.
*Photo: Norbert Hess*

Left to right: Nesuhi Ertegun, Jerry Wexler, Carl Gardener, Dub Jones, Billy Guy, Cornel Gunter, Ahmet Ertegun, (seated) Jerry Leiber, Mike Stoller, 1959.

The Cadillacs. *Top:* Earl Carroll; *bottom* (left to right): Earl Wade, Bobby Philips, Charles Brooks, Laverne Drake.

Sonny Forriest 1962.
*Photo: Kurt Mohr*

Young Jessie.

*Right:* (Left to right):
Earl Carroll, Dub Jones,
Carl Gardener, Billy Guy.
*Centre:* The Coasters with
Adolphi Jacobs.
*Bottom:* The Coasters.

The Coasters. Left to right: Dub Jones, Carl Gardener, Cornel Gunter, Billy Guy.

Cornel Gunter's Coasters. Left to right: Cornel Gunter, Nat Wilson, Bobby Stregar.

Leiber and Stoller also produced: *Top:* Isley Brothers, Linda Hopkins. *Centre:* Ruth Brown, Lavern Baker. *Bottom:* Exciters, Sammy Turner.

Top Notes, Billy Storm, and, according to him, Bobby Darin. He was also contracted to play rhythm guitar on several Drifters sessions and 'Shoppin' for Clothes' which he may well have loathed. Making a record with four instruments must have been anathema to him particularly when two of these, including his own contribution, are barely discernible. Nevertheless, by 1960, 'Shoppin' for Clothes' was probably the closest anyone involved in making pop music had come to fine art: another five years would elapse before any such accolade could be directed at The Beatles or Spector himself. The latter's hesitant guitar playing is heard more prominently on 'Thumbin' a Ride' but a third song from the same session, 'Dogface', remains unissued.

In common with all popular music of the day, 'Shoppin' for Clothes' met with little serious acclaim when it was issued. In 1973 it was reissued in Britain. It did not sell even then but some records are always destined to be way ahead of their time. On this occasion, however, the name of the unfortunate Kent Harris—'Cops and Robbers' was snapped up by Bo Diddley who also claimed to have written it—now appeared in its rightful place as composer. In 1962 Progressive Music, Atlantic's publishing arm, was purchased by Aberbach's Hill and Range company who, in 1967, bought American Music from Sylvester Cross. If 'Clothesline' is ever reissued (perhaps by Liberty who have made some of Eddie Cochran's Crest material available), Harris can be sure of receiving royalties for that, and 'Shoppin' for Clothes', from the same source.

After making 'Shoppin' for Clothes', Leiber and Stoller took a brief rest from recording The Coasters who, in December 1960, returned to Los Angeles where they cut 'Ridin Hood' under the supervision of Lester Sill and Lee Hazlewood. The two men had, of course, collaborated before. Hazlewood had produced a great many atmospheric instrumental hits for Duane Eddy and, apart from the aforementioned 3-Trey, Atlantic had previously distributed another label devoted to Sill and Hazlewood's productions. East–West. Their first Coasters record was certainly a good one. They were not particularly imaginative but 'Ridin' Hood' has all the usual ingredients of the best Coasters records. Dub Jones has some goofy lines and Steve Douglas replicates King Curtis with brief phrases between the words which the group sing with their customary gusto. The song itself was of particular interest and introduced another young composer, Dallas Frazier.

An important writer, Frazier is one of several white Southerners whose own records—too much like r & b for country fans, too country for black record-buyers and yet often alien to the general mainstream of popular music—are less successful than his songs for other artists. His early lyrics, which drew heavily on a humorous teenage lexicon, bear favourable comparison with those of Jerry Leiber and, to some extent, he was absorbed into the history of The Coasters who also recorded two more of his songs, 'She's a Yum Yum' and Mohair Sam'. Born in Spiro, Oklahoma in 1939, Frazier's family moved to the cottonfields of Bakersfield, California when he was ten. Two years later he won a talent contest sponsored by Ferlin Husky who introduced him to Capitol records. The label issued some precocious kiddie-style novelties including 'Love life at 14' (2895), 'Space Command' (2813), and an EP, 'My Birthday comes on Christmas'. Listening to these, it is almost inconceivable that Dallas heard any blues or country music before he reached fourteen but perhaps he genuinely preferred 'Jingle Bells'. Thankfully he went back to school. By 1959 he had stopped imitating Mel Blanc but still read comics. His first song-writing success, a teenage talking blues called 'Alley Oop', topped the U.S. charts by The Hollywood Argyles (Lute 5905), in 1960 and, for a while, the strip cartoon character became as famous as 'Charlie Brown'. While Leiber and Stoller were producing records in a lavish, carefully rehearsed fashion, 'Alley Oop' demonstrated just how casually an adolescent group could wind up with a million seller. Frazier had written the words on a paper sack. Someone, possibly Kim Fowley, taps a waste-paper basket while drummer, Sandy Nelson, who screams twice, chinks a cider bottle which lead 'singer', Gary Paxton, had emptied. 'You could tell Gary had been drinking hard cider,' said Nelson. 'Listen to the fadeout, we had to hold him up.' Paxton took comic novelties a stage further when, in 1961, he produced Bobby Pickett who narrated 'Monster Mash', 'Monster's Holiday', 'Monster Motion', and other gory slices from the same cadaver. These depended more on Pickett's ability to imitate Boris Karloff than any allegiance to The Coasters but there were those who thought they were the next best comedy records around and the group may well have helped in creating the opportunities for marketing this kind of material to a teenage audience.

The Hollywood Argyles, a makeshift combination to begin with, had no more hits although the titles to some of their later records—'A Gun-Totin' Crittur called Jack' (Lute 5908), 'You been Torturing Me' (Paxley 752), 'Long Hair, Unsquare Dude named Jack' (Chattahoochee 691)—suggest that Frazier's inventive mind was still at work. No one can touch him for song titles; witness the comparatively recent compositions 'The Conspiracy of Homer Jones' (Capitol 2402) or 'The Birthmark Henry Thompson talks about' (RCA 9881), both of which he recorded himself. With the demise of The Hollywood Argyles, Frazier recorded his own songs for Jamie, Musikon, Mercury, and Capitol—enjoying his only hit with 'Elvira' (Capitol 5560) in 1966—and wrote some of the sixties' best pop records including 'The Son of Hickory Holler's Tramp' by O. C. Smith (Columbia 44425), 'Mohair Sam' for Charlie Rich (Smash 1993), and, less successful though just as enjoyable, 'Ridin' Hood' by The Coasters:

*'Once upon a time there was a chick all dressed in red*
*A swingin' down the path, a hood was hanging on her head.'*

Many of the neat, colloquial touches in Frazier's updated nursery rhyme suggest that he would have been an ideal soulmate for Mike Stoller; no one else came quite as close to Jerry Leiber's eloquent vernacularism:

*'She motivated groovy like they do in Hollywood*
*when out behind the trees there jumped a great big ugly wolf*
*"Pardon me" he said real cool. "Why make the scene alone"*
*a crazy chick like you should have a han'some chaperone.'*

Like many of The Coaster's songs, 'Ridin' Hood' was concluded with a moral ('If you dig chicks in red you better change your colour to green'), and Frazier had clearly set out to emulate the material for which the group were now immediately recognized. It is probable that the general feel of 'Ridin' Hood' was based on 'Run, Red, Run', just as other Frazier compositions, 'Alley Oop' and 'Mohair Sam', have obvious affinities with 'Searchin'' and 'Along Came Jones'. Back in New York for their first session of 1961, The Coasters made what is generally thought to be their last real classic, 'Little Egypt', and, another tune of less repute, 'Girls, Girls, Girls', both, of course, Leiber–Stoller compositions.

*'Girls, Girls, Girls, Girls,*
*Gettin' on buses, gettin' outa taxis, walkin' an' wigglin' by*
*Yeah, Yeah, Yeah, Girls,*
*In tight sweaters, in short dresses, Oh pretty Lord I could cry*
*I'm just a red blooded boy an' I can't stop thinkin' about girls.'*

What could be simpler than that? Billy Guy invests this lucid distillation of teenage obsession with a weird and decidedly manic sneakiness. If voices could cop a feel no girl could play the record without experiencing some odd sensations. As it was, 'Girls, Girls, Girls' did not climb above the lower-most rungs of the Hot Hundred and disappeared after two weeks on the chart. It wasn't *that* bad but the flip—the same song only faster—was obviously no help to the consumer who may well have resented such shoddy manipulation.

In the late forties, Red Ingle and The Natural Seven recorded 'Moe Zart's Turkey Trot' (Capitol 13045), a jokey piano instrumental (based on Mozart's *Rondo Alla turca*), in which one of the Natural Seven, 'Frank the Turk' declares:

*'Step right up gents and see Little Eva, it's all free and on the inside*
*She'll shake and quake like a tromped on-snake.'*

The couplet is not dissimilar to the introduction to 'Little Egypt' and although Stoller had not heard of Ingle, 'Moe Zart's Turkey Trot' combined classical music, piano, and a spoof—all characteristics of which he was particularly fond —and the record might conceivably have buried itself in his subconscious. The rest of 'Little Egypt' was wholly and peremptorily original:

*'Step right up folks an' see Little Egypt do a famous dance of the pyramids*
*She walks, she talks, she crawls on her belly like a reptile*
*Just one thin dime, one tenth of a dollar, step right up folks.*

*I went an' bought myself a ticket an' I sat down in the very first row*
*they pulled the curtain up an' when they turned the spotlight way down low*
*Little Egypt came out strippin' wearin' nothin' but a button an' a bow.*

*She had a ruby on her tummy an' a diamond big as Texas on her toe*
*she let her hair down an' she did the hootchy kootchy real slow*
*when she did a special number on a zebra skin I thought she'd stop the show.*

*She did a triple somersault and when she hit the ground*
*she winked at the audience and then she turned around*
*she had a picture of a cowboy tattoed on her spine*
*sayin' "Phoenix, Arizona, Nineteen Forty-Nine".*

*Yeah, but let me tell you people Little Egypt doesn't dance there any more*
*she's too busy moppin' an' a takin' care of shoppin' at the store*
*cos we've got seven kids an' all day long they crawl around the floor.'*

Unlike 'Shoppin' for Clothes' (how do you whistle a duologue?), 'Little Egypt' was not only thoroughly amusing but instantly hummable. There are many deft touches. The group drag out the final syllable of each line, totally mesmerized by events on stage; Curtis' stuttering breaks are as fresh and commanding as ever; the guitarist plays a splendid little coda that is absolutely right and Billy Guy snorts 'Yeah' with the contemptuous air of one who can now enjoy a sinusful of G-string every night of the week. If this book had a few pictures of 'Little Egypt' wearing nothing but a button and a bow it might well be sold under the counter in plain wrappers; the record was received somewhat gingerly as well.

An instrumental called 'The Stripper' (David Rose—MGM 13064), topped the charts the following year but no one who sang about such things stood very much chance of selling records in the era of lachrymose ballads and high school pop slop. Apart from Presley's 'Jailhouse Rock',

Leiber's propensity for prisons, racetracks, and blue-light diners was not the stuff of which colossal hits were made. By the time he got around to strip-joints, his prurience was still far from being universally acceptable. The attitude of radio stations received no press coverage but Billy Guy believes 'Little Egypt' was subject to a widespread ban throughout the South. It rivalled the very best Coasters discs in every department and nothing else can account for its comparatively poor chart progress. 'Little Egypt' was the last of Leiber and Stoller's positively brilliant composition/productions for The Coasters or, indeed, anyone else.

* * *

Apart from Ben E. King and The Drifters (whose records are discussed in the author's book, 'The Drifters: The Rise and Fall of the Black Vocal Group'),[4] Leiber and Stoller's songs and/or productions for other Atlantic and Atco artists—The Crescendos, Young Jessie, Wynonie Harris, Clyde McPhatter, Ray Charles, Chris Conner, Joe Turner, Lonnie Donegan, King Curtis—were less than consistently wonderful. To say more than this would grant an unwarranted importance to records which, for the most part, few people heard and fewer still bought. I think it instructive however to dwell briefly on a handful of discs which stand out by virtue of qualities which characterize the best Coasters' records. Leiber's charismatic sense of humour was, for example, clearly imprinted on a number of excellent sides by Atlantic's foremost songstresses, LaVern Baker and Ruth Brown, the only women for whom he and Stoller regularly wrote material. Truly big, black and beautiful, both possessed deep, warm, broken-note voices with a masculine timbre which enabled them to sing earthy lyrics without any hint of coyness. The material Leiber and Stoller gave to Ruth Brown was nonetheless erratic. 'Lucky Lips' (Atlantic 1125), a computerized ditty as trivial as pure pop invariably is, was written with the charts in mind. It was necessary to break Ruth, a huge star with a devoted black following, into the lucrative white pop market and so long as she made the top thirty ('Lucky Lips' hit number 26 in 1957) the archives could go to hell. Jerry Leiber probably kicked himself all the way to the bank. 'Jack O' Diamonds' (Atlantic 2026), the bouncy saga of a gambling man, was equally inconsequential (and it also made the Hot Hundred) but the reverse, 'I Can't Hear a Word You Say', ranks high among their wittiest twelve—bar blues:

*'He handed me his card and said "My name is Poppa Joe"*
*said "I'm a talent scout baby, I can do things for you."*

The poseur, Poppa Joe, is really after a bit of the other:

*'He said, "You may not know it from the look of my clothes*
*but I taught Nat King Cole everything he knows*
*meet me in the back booth of The Big Beat Bar*
*I might just decide to make you a recordin' star."'*

Ruth repeatedly offers the rebuff contained in the title of the song and a back-up female vocal group hiss 'Bigshot, Bigshot' with some malevolence. The melody is not unlike that of 'Framed' while Stoller's bone-crushing orchestration is redolent of a gangster movie soundtrack. Ultimately, it's a parody of a parody; the ghetto equivalent of 'All American Boy' ('Come here cat, I'm gonna make you a star') and doubtless the more realistically seedy picture. 'Papa Daddy' (Atl 2035), a dirty old man whose activities are performed to a crashing Bo Diddley rhythm, is another of Leiber's hilarious characters:

*'Papa Daddy said I'm gonna kiss you*
*Papa Daddy did what he said he'd do*
*Papa Daddy sat me on his knee, said, "Little girl I'm 63*
*but I'm a better man than Stag O Lee."'*

Fortunately for programme directors, Ruth Brown's voice, mature and laced with experience, was enough to dispel the blatant suggestion of child molester.

Their songs for LaVern Baker, 'Whipper Snapper' (Atl 1189), 'Don Juan', and 'Saved' (Atl 2099)—a top forty hit in 1961—seriously rivalled those for Ruth Brown. 'Saved', probably their first gospel number since 'That's what The Good Book Says', is a particularly jubilant excursion. While the double shuffle beat, handclapping and antiphonal chorus reek of the church, the lyrics maintain the high-spirited humour more appropriate to secular composition:

*'I used to smoke, I used to drink*
*I used to smoke, drink, and dance the hoochy koo*
*but now I'm standing on this corner praying for me and you.'*

Gospel singers are not always the innocents they seem: LaVern sings as if she's going to have a few jars just as soon as the session's over. The song was chosen by Presley to open his 1968 TV special.

'You're The Boss' (Atlantic 2090), a duet between LaVern Baker and Jimmy Ricks, is another of Leiber and Stoller's little gems. If Cole Porter had been black he might well have written something like this:

(Ricks) *'Baby you're a genius when it comes to cooking up some chili sauce*
(Baker) *but in the middle of the night when the moon is shining bright*
(both) *You're The Boss.'*

Genius is slotting the word into a song and creating the impression that it rhymes with 'boss' and 'chili sauce'. It's really daring; rather like using 'concrete' and 'rose' in 'Spanish Harlem' (which Leiber and Phil Spector wrote for Ben E. King—Atco 6185) and making those words seem like the most natural combination in the world.

Better yet were two sessions which Leiber and Stoller produced for The Isley Brothers. 'Teach Me How To Shimmy' (Atl 2092), made in December 1960, was far more than another dance record. The lead sings with a hard, crystalline edge and the request becomes a threat. If he can't learn to shimmy in time for the dance, Chico will steal his chick and there'll be one hell of a rumble. The menacing atmosphere is pointed up by startling original string and percussion patterns and the voices of the other Isleys provide the rich sort of cushion more commonly heard behind The Coasters' Billy Guy. The following April, The Coasters revived the song in Los Angeles where, once again, they were produced by Lee Hazlewood and Lester Sill who, it must be said, lacked the maestros' touch. The Coasters version was nothing out of the ordinary, losing all the complexity and subtlety of that by The Isley Brothers whose next single, 'Shine on Harvest Moon' (Atl 2100) was really quite extraordinary.

Leiber and Stoller's attitude towards *songs* is complex. Stoller once remarked that he didn't like them yet their production of 'Zing went the Strings of My heart', perhaps one of the most idyllic and unrealistic of all Tin Pan Alley lyrics, is very nearly respectable. Possessed of a certain old-fashioned polish and formality, it would not be out of place on 'Family Favourites' or any other horripilant vehicle for family entertainment. Their interpretation of other old songs was often very different. Like The Coasters' 'Sweet Georgia Brown' there was nothing elegant about their production of 'Shine on Harvest Moon'. It can only be appreciated by blocking out the words with their traditionally silly connotations and regarding the melody as something inherently interesting to be worked on and elaborated. All sentimentality is dispelled as The Isleys tear away at the bar-room tawdriness of the tune. Leiber and Stoller must have sweated for an eternity. It was mangled, stamped on, abused, and compartmentalized. The old, orthodox cliches of Tin Pan Alley are juxtaposed with rock 'n' roll's most diverting tricks; King Curtis blows a ripping tenor solo hard up against weepy violins while the groups' ear-splitting falsetto wails shred the melody into barely recognizable pieces. A mind-blowing record by any criteria, 'Shine on Harvest Moon' caused very little excitement when issued but genius shines out of every groove and it's unquestionably one of Leiber and Stoller's most transfixing productions. The reverse, 'Standing on The Dance Floor', a raw and phrenetic secularisation of The Sensational Nightingales 'Standing at The Judgement' (Peacock 1804), was only less than stunning while 'Your Old Lady' (Atlantic 2110) also had some fine moments. As one might expect from writer's credits which include the pseudonym, 'Glick', there is a blunt and humorous couplet:

*'I don't want to cut you 'cos you're my friend*
*but your old lady, Lord she's the livin' end.'*

Finally, in 1962, Leiber and Stoller wrote 'Some Other Guy' (Atlantic 2142) for Richie Barrett. A muffled scorcher based on the electric piano beat of 'What'd I Say', it was something of a seminal record in the British r & b boom. The flip, 'Tricky Dicky', just might have been veiled political prophesy but more likely just the last of their prison songs. 'Tricky Dicky ya done bust out.'

Eight years had elapsed since CBS had banned The Robins' 'Riot in Cell Block No. 9' for fear that it might have touched off prison unrest. Eight years on and very few of Leiber and Stoller's most intriguing records for The Isley Brothers, Ruth Brown, or Richie Barrett had sold in any great quantity. The musical climate of the early sixties was still not sufficiently advanced to incorporate all Leiber and Stoller's more unconservative approaches to pop music and they would soon subjugate their talents to the commercial demands of the period.

* * *

Late in 1961, Cornelius Gunter left The Coasters to join Dinah Washington's revue. Shortly after this, he embarked on a parasitic but lucrative career by forming the first of several permutations which he cheekily called The Coasters. One such group, including former members of The Penguins—Teddy Harper, Randolph Jones, and Dexter Tisby—recorded with him for Challenge in 1964 but the record ('Wishful Thinking' c & w 'Key to your Heart') was credited to Gunter only. In November 1966 he toured Britain with a fresh set of phoney Coasters including Nathaniel Wilson, late of The Hollywood Saxons and The Shields (he sang on their top ten hit of 1958, 'You Cheated', Tender 513), and Bobby Stegar who had previously recorded for Buddha. The trio—a fourth member, McKinley Travis, was serving in Vietnam—were an excellent imitation of the real thing with a far from perfunctory act. Gunter appeared resplendent in a silver lurex pyjama suit and lashings of matching nail varnish and eye make-up. Undaunted by cries of 'Who's the woman?' he ploughed through all The Coasters hits without lisping and revealed a personality at least as large as Little Richard and Mohammed Ali combined. All this five years before glitter-rock; chalk up another first for The Coasters.

Gunter and his friends subsequently performed all over the U.S.A., despite management problems with H. B. Barnum who filed suit against them in the Los Angeles Superior Court in 1971. The suit, which named Gunter as principal of The Coasters, stated that they entered into a representation with Barnum on 6 April 1971 and broke it 20 July. The three-year contract called for Barnum to get ten per cent of The Coasters earning through $7,500 a week, fifteen per cent up to $15,000, and twenty per cent of all weekly Coaster earnings over $15,000. He claimed the group owed him $60,000 in personal management fees and asked for $300,000 punitive damages and an injunction preventing The Coasters from entering into any other personal management contract without his approval. The result was not publicized but Gunter's fake Coasters clearly weren't working for peanuts and, much to Carl Gardner's understandable annoyance, they seemed destined to survive:

'We own the name, Billy Guy an' myself. We hired Cornelius for five years but he wasn't an original. He hadda lotta nerve an' just went back to California an' formed his own group with guys who'd never sang with The Coasters at all. There's still not too much we can do about it either, like goin' to court. We could go an' get injunctions after injunctions in every single state but it's gonna cost money....'

Gunter's place in the proper Coasters was taken by Earl 'Speedo' Carroll who remains with the group today. He's still a rocker. The other Coasters now wear Afros and denims but Carroll likes wide, baggy suits and still affects the slick, shiny process which his teenage fans had admired when he was lead singer of The Cadillacs. Shy but manifestly likeable, he greets each question with an engaging grin: 'When I was a young kid I used to have a hair dig—it used to shoot straight up kinda steeple-like. We were playing outside an armoury an' there was a big bombshell out in front and the kids said "Speedo—there's your Torpedo" so that's where Speedo came from.'

Born in New York City in 1937, Carroll left Metropolitan Vocational High School in 1953 and formed The Carnations with Bobby Phillips, LaVern Drake, and Gus Willingham. A little later they added John 'Poppa' Clark from The Five Crowns and changed their name to The Cadillacs whose story has been well documented in the American journal of group archaeology, 'Bim Bam Boom'.[5] 'We were discovered in a hallway singin' an' havin' a little taste of sherry,' remembered Carroll. 'We had the whole building tied up an' Lover Patterson introduced us to Esther Navarro in his house on 118th Street, 8th Avenue, the heart of the ghetto. We had to be at our sharpest, 'cos he had a young lady comin' by who knew Jerry Blaine.' An ex-bandleader and owner of numerous r & b labels, Blaine had previously been introduced to The Orioles by another shrewd Jewish lady, Deborah Chessler. In much the same way, Esther Navarro brought him the Cadillacs whose records soon appeared on Josie with her name in the composing credits although Carroll claimed tartly, 'Esther was our producer, no way a writer.' They began in October 1954 with 'I wonder Why' (765), a fast workout with peppy bass/falsetto harmonies and a heavy backbeat. While the groups' slow ballads, like the reverse, 'Gloria', find favour with American collectors today, The Cadillacs preferred a faster, harder style apparently consistent with one of the most choreographed of all early rock 'n' roll acts. Indeed, European enthusiasts regard the group as one of the premier rock 'n' roll quartets, perhaps second only to The Coasters in terms of authenticity. No one put any strings behind The Cadillacs; just a thundering beat from guitarist Skeeter Best and Jesse Powell, the saxophonist who helped to boot a lot of their discs into the East coast best-sellers. Their biggest hit, 'Speedoo' (785, number thirty in 1955), a perfect crystallization of the uptempo New York vocal group sound, was little more than a private joke for themselves and their fans—'Some folks call me Speedo but my real name is Mr. Earl'—but the tune was appealing enough to attract enormous national sales. Carroll's voice had little social context. There were no fierce black inflections nor any trace of awesome key-juggling. It was light, happy, and patently youthful. Synoptically, he was very good indeed; his very lack of distinction provided the model for a great many street-corner teams, both black and white. 'Gloria', for example, was revived by The Passions, Vito and The Salutation, The Escorts, and The Channels.

While West Coast groups employed the humour of the blues, those based in The East had a more serious harmonic tradition. Apart from 'Gloria', songs like The Lovenotes 'United' (Holiday 2605), The Five Satins 'In the Still of The Night' (Ember 1005), and The Cadillacs 'Dum de dum dum' (Jubilee LP 5009), will be familiar to sixties' soul-buyers from versions by The Jive Five, The Intruders, and The Drifters. In addition, particular harmonic sequences have long been incorporated on a variety of different group recordings. Carroll provides some examples: 'There was a group known as The Regals managed by Bobby Schiffman whose father ran "The Apollo". They hadda tune out called "Water Boilin' Baby" (Atlantic 1062) an' we kinda fell in love with the background they were doing so we took out the "Wop wah" an' "Doo we doo" an' put it to "Speedo" which was very successful for us. The Spaniels took "Stormy Weather" from us. We were on a show together up in Connecticut an' I wondered why they kept telling us, "Sing that one more time, jus' one more time eh?" We had a fine arrangement an' y'know we's proud to sing it. Next thing I knew it was out on the street by Pookie Hudson and The Spaniels, same harmonies, same arrangement, same everythin'. We also took a pattern off The Coasters with "Peekaboo, I'm watching you".'

A spooky rocker, 'Peekaboo' (846), which made the top thirty in 1958, was The Cadillacs' last big hit and it marked a radical change in material. Inspired by The Coasters' Orwellian vision of the future, 'The Shadow Knows', it was succeeded by a number of pure comic novelties—'Jay Walker' (857), 'Please Mr. Johnson' (861), and 'Bad Dan McGoon' (870)—in which the material was practically an infringement of Leiber and Stoller's copyright and the bass voice emulated Dub Jones. The Cadillacs belated comic flair had proved that Carroll was a natural conscript for The Coasters who promptly recorded his own composition, 'Just like Me', in September 1961. While The Hollies covered it for English consumption, the nursery-based rhyme had very little to commend it and the session from which it came—the first to be held in Atlantic's new studios at 1841 Broadway—was not an auspicious debut. 'My Babe' was used as an uninteresting album filler while 'Bad Blood', a not uncommon medical expression in blues lore, failed to live up to the promise of its title. The Coasters were now on the way down and even a good record like 'The Climb' was unable to revive their flagging fortunes:

*'Cheek to Cheek, ah toes to toes*
*here's a dance you can do all the time*
*knees to knees, nose to nose*
*hardly move an' you're doin' the climb.'*

It was a slow, deliberately laconic chant, unusual, effective and a lot of fun. 'I loved "The Climb",' said Stoller, 'but it was originally much funnier. It was called "The Slime" at first and it was a take-off of all the dance crazes. Jerry Wexler said "Yuk! That's disgusting. Slime ugh! You can't put that on a record. Not slime man, you gotta change the title." So we went back in the studio and over dubbed the word "climb". It was funny as "The Slime"—"The Climb" doesn't mean anything.'

As usual, Stoller was right. Compared to 'Slime', the substitution certainly lacked saliency. Following fast on the heels of 'The Twist', 'The Wah Watusi', and 'The Waddle', trade papers reviewed 'The Climb' as another mindless dance craze and any satirical quality went unrecognized. It meant little more in terms of sales although a black group (not The Coasters) revived the song in one of Elvis Presley's films, 'Viva Las Vegas'. 'The Climb' also introduced The Coasters current guitarist, Thomas Palmer, a 35-year-old Texan whose credentials include work with the orchestras of Sonny Thompson and Lloyd Price. 'Bull Tick Waltz', from 'The Climb' session, was a literally fantastic variation on the already improbable theme of Burl Ives' 'Ugly Bug Ball'.

*'The bugs in my bed threw a party last night*
*they were dancin' the bull-tick waltz*
*a stink bug crawled in with a small jug of cider*
*his arms around the hip of a black widow spider....'*

Undeniably imaginative, it may nonetheless have been Leiber and Stoller's silliest novelty (though I've not heard 'Happy Little Snapdragon') and when it failed to impress Walt Disney or anyone else, they produced just one more dog and then gave up.

'The P.T.A.' (Parent–Teacher Association) was written by Paul Evans who is chiefly despised for his hit of 1959, 'Seven Little Girls sitting in The Back Seat' (Guaranteed 200). That same stultiloquence infects 'The P.T.A.' where three other little girls holler 'Hey, hey—at the P.T.A.' in stuck-pig voices. A monumentally vacuous song, it was unworthy of anyone's attention. 'I'm not sure why we produced it,' said Stoller, 'It wasn't our song, it was just an imitation of what The Coasters had done a number of years before. We stopped producing them after that.'

Apart from 'Little Egypt' and 'Shoppin' for Clothes', Leiber and Stoller's last two years with The Coasters had produced no really memorable record. There was little sense of involvement in the tales which they had once told with such enthusiasm and several numbers were devoid of the strong commitment with which their ideas had previously been expressed. Without these qualities records like 'The P.T.A.' 'Bad Blood' and 'Bull Tick Waltz' were little more than distressingly silly pop tunes. Superficially, they shared the same content, style, and imagination which had characterized far better Coasters records but that mysteriously vital creative spark was missing, perhaps extinguished by repetition. Leiber and Stoller had grown stale.

Their departure from the recording studios, left Atlantic with the question of what to do with The Coasters until their seven year contract (ratified at the time of 'Charlie Brown') expired in 1966. It was a problem they never really solved. The group made another six singles for Atlantic and each involved different writers and producers. The first of these, two live recordings made at The Apollo Theatre with The King Curtis band, was easily the best. The Coasters celebrated Earl Carroll's recruitment with an old Cadillacs number, 'Speedo is Back' (Josie 836); suitably amended, audience reaction suggests it was a real crowd pleaser:

*'Gee Speedo we miss you so*
*Now it's good to be back in town.*
*Cadillac—diamond ring*
*since ah been with The Coasters ah got everythin'.'*

'Tain't nothin' to Me', the other 'Apollo' song, was written by Lover Patterson, the strawboss behind The Five Crowns. In all respects, it was truly a black comedy; a man approaches man at bar, insults his girl-friend ('I'd rather have a hot seat in Sing Sing Prison than to sit by her on that stool') and winds up on the floor with a bullet in his head. Very much a visual experience, it lost a great deal in the audile transition. Doubtless the group camped it up on-stage, pulling guns, rolling their eyes, and aping any number of emotions like the vaudeville actors they really were. The exclusively black audience thought it was a riot but on the record we hear them falling about without quite knowing why. Nevertheless, white kids bought sufficient copies to make it the group's last national hit for eight years; Dub Jones' accent, deep, droopy, and thick enough to bump into, was evidently funny enough on its own.

The Coasters followed 'Tain't Nothing to Me' with a slew of r & b revivals: The Clovers 'Lovey Dovey' (Atlantic 1022), The Robins 'I must be Dreamin'', The Drifters 'Money Honey' (Atlantic 1006) and, one song everyone took to be a revival, 'Let's go get stoned'. A fine song by Tamla writers, Nick Ashford and Valerie Simpson, The Coasters made it in April 1965 but Atlantic failed to release it at the time and, a year later, Ray Charles topped the r & b chart with his version (ABC 10808), which was certainly no better. But as pleasant as many of these sides undoubtedly were, the fact had to be faced: The Coasters were no longer a hot property. Each new Coasters single had been a prime contender for air-play on pop stations but the English invasion—led by The Beatles about whom The Coasters sang on the execrable 'Wild One'—trampled all over their more deserving later issues, most of which are now hard to locate. Gregory Carroll, who produced 'Wild One', was not related to Earl but he had a long involvement with vocal groups including experience as a founder member of The Four Buddies who, as The Metronomes, had backed up Little Esther on Savoy when The Robins left The Johnny Otis revue in 1950. Three years later, he replaced second tenor George Nelson in The Orioles but arguably his greatest moment arrived in 1963 when he produced and co-authored Doris Troy's top ten hit 'Just one Look' (Atlantic 2188). 'I must be Dreaming', Carroll's other Coasters production, deserved a similar placing. The ten-year-old Robins number was given a raunchier beat with a blues guitar solo instead of Gil Bernal's saxophone and the final verse is missing altogether. As a ghost from the early fifties it was a gas but, by 1964, funny rock 'n' roll records were a total anachronism and 'I must be Dreaming' will have seemed pretty cobwebbed to post-Beatle ears.

With only one release per year, The Coasters busied themselves with Coca-Cola jingles and picked up New Yorker, Vernon Harrell, who deputized for Billy Guy during the latter's periodic attempts at solo stardom. Once a perennial, if virtually anonymous, inhabitant of the top thirty, Guy now slipped from label to label: Double L, ABC–Paramount, Chalco, Verve, Sew City, and, more recently, All Platinum. Some of his solo records were heralded as '*Billboard*'s Pick of the week' and others were lost in the flood. None were hits to speak of and he was always sufficiently close at hand to replace Harrell by the time a new Coasters session came around. In 1965, he helped produce his own composition, 'Crazy Baby'. A regional hit in Philadelphia, it also received airplay over WHCB in Detroit and KYOK in Houston but soul records with vibes and a clomping beat were legion and some attention to the flip, a funny Ertegun composition, 'Bell Bottom Slacks and a Chinese Kimono (she's my little spodee-o)', might then have been preferable. It certainly gladdened the hearts of the Coasters fans although 'Crazy Baby' would now be an odds-on favourite with discotheque dancers in the North of England.

The group entered Atlantic's studios for the last time in January 1966. Produced by King Curtis, they recorded two judicious selections, 'She's a yum yum', a Dallas Frazier song previously given to Charlie Rich, and 'Saturday Night Fish Fry', a prehistoric jump blues popularized by Louis Jordan (Decca 24725) in 1949. As a contemporary concession the accompaniment was thick and beefy but there was no mistaking the vocal interplay, King's yakety tenor solo or the general *joie de vivre*:

(Billy Guy) *'Now over in the corner was a beat up grand*
(Dub Jones) *played by a big fat piano man*
(Harmony) *They were rockin', they were rockin' in there.'*

Ten years on and eighteen hits later, The Coasters were still rockin'. It was a grand way to go.

* * *

If Louis Jordan's riotous and often ribald jump blues was the funniest music which blacks could offer during the forties, many second-generation r & b stars were influenced by The Coasters. Very often it's difficult to be specific. Who, for example, would have thought Curtis Mayfield's epic rock 'n' soul records might not have happened without them? Mayfield who left The Impressions to become one of the first black super-stars of the seventies, had this to say about his musical beginnings: 'Around 1955 I got into r & b and rock 'n' roll. I started to like all kinds of music even classical, but I especially loved The Coasters. We started a group called The Alphatones and learned all their songs ... the Chicago singing groups like The Spaniels and

The Dells really knocked me out but I'd say The Coasters were my biggest inspiration.'[6]

The influence of The Coasters' Atlantic sound on particular records is far more tangible. Disembodied bass voices, ersatz King Curtis solos, the tone and colour of Billy Guy's distinctive baritone, Stoller's alley piano rhythms ... all these techniques and characteristics were slavishly copied by a host of other writers, producers, and performers. Ignoring straight-forward cover versions, there are probably more quasi-Coasters' records than donkey's footprints on Blackpool beach.

Although Ray Stevens string of lunatic hits were clear proof of his allegiance—his revival of 'Along Came Jones' (Monument 1150) made the top 30 in 1969—and Joe Tex's 'Charlie Brown Got Expelled' (Ace 559) was a brilliant facsimile, most imitations were not unnaturally by groups. While it would be nugatory to list hundreds of indigestible names, many achieved some degree of popularity. There were The Hollywood Hurricanes, The Pleasures, The Halos —'Nag' (7 Arts 709) made the top 30 in 1961—The Jiving Juniors, The Sevilles—'Charlena' (JC 116) was another 1961 chart entrant—The Commodores ... the list is endless. Some, like The Hollywood Argyles, sang about the heroes of popular culture or other communal figures and experiences. Hence The Cap-Tans 'Revenue Man' (Loop 100); The La-Rells 'Public Transportation' (Robbee 114) in which a bass voice intones, 'Please move to the rear'; The Delacardos 'Mr Dillon' (U.A. 310), hero of the then popular television western, 'Gunsmoke'; and as late as 1972, 'Lady Godiva' by a white aggregation, Dr. Hook and The Medicine Band. The arrangement by Shel Silverstein recreated The Coasters' sound more faithfully than all previous attempts. If Leiber and Stoller ever heard the song they must have paused for a moment and wondered when they'd written it.

As far as black groups were concerned, Frank Zappa reinforces the belief that a comic approach was the main distinction between those from the East and those based in California: 'The West Coast music had a sense of humour but the stuff from the East was kinda desperate. Group music was brought to California by black people from Texas and the ghetto situation in L.A. wasn't as nasty as it was in Harlem, so it developed a different aura—do you know The Coasters "Shoppin' for Clothes"? That's the sort of thing I mean."[7] Whatever the social conditions—and Zappa's explanation is as good as any—Los Angeles spawned a vast number of group novelty records, a phenomenon in which the early success of Leiber and Stoller's records with The Robins and The Coasters played a significant role. 'Searchin'' was particularly popular. A shrill or sneaky lead, an indolent bass voice and ludicrously simple lyrics became the staple ingredients of a black novelty disc. Many were concerned with food; The Marathons 'Peanut Butter' (Arvee 5027) and Ronnie and Joey's 'Frozen Dinners' (Little Star 106), both produced by H. B. Barnum; 'Chocolate Pudding' from Abaco Dream (A & M 1160) and 'Hot Tamales' by the Righteous Brothers ('Moonglow'), one half of whom, Bill Medley, had previously sung with The Paramours on 'Prison Break' (Smash 1701), a number plainly inspired by 'Riot in Cell Block No. 9.' 'Pork Chops', 'Black-eyed Peas' ... *et hoc.*

'Western Movies' (Demon 1508) and 'Hully Gully' (Arvee 562), exceptions to the gastronomic theme but firmly based on that innovatory piano rhythm, were big hits in 1958 and 1960 for The Olympics, another Los Angeles group whose chart record eventually overtook The Coasters. Although originally made by Don and Dewey, 'Big Boy Pete' (Arvee 595)—the wryly amusing adventures of a ghetto hustler—also dealt with a scenario familiar to Coasters' fans. The voice of The Olympics' lead singer, Walter Ward, was closely modelled on Billy Guy's most unintelligible shriek while their producer, Fred Smith, rivalled Leiber and Stoller in his commitment and devotion. Randy Wood, Smith's employer at Mirwood records, explains: 'Fred is extremely creative. He was originally taught to play the clarinet by Buddy Collette who urged him to get into arranging but his long suit is in production. He doesn't write songs, he writes records as pure commodity. He'll lay down tracks with a constant rhythmic pattern from James Carmichael on piano and then he'll stack horns three different times at three different levels. They're impossible to duplicate but categorically he couldn't go in and make the same record twice. A lot of work goes into them but the records have a spontaneity. I don't know if anyone else could make hit records with The Olympics, I seriously doubt it.' Just to clinch the connection, The Olympics also revived The Robins 'Loop de Loop Mambo' and called it 'Loop de Loop Limbo' (Tri-Disc LP 1001). It was credited to Leibert and Stroller!

Almost without exception, these imitations lacked Leiber's very special sense of humour (you couldn't bust a gut over 'My baby loves the western movies') and tributes of this kind were rarely able to stretch beyond the refinements of the basic approach. They all display unmistakably Coasterish traits but that's where they end. It was impossible to improve The Coasters sound; it was already as perfect as could be. Unlike those made by their imitators, most of The Coasters' records improve with age. It's probably the finest tribute one can pay.

CHAPTER SIX

# WHAT ABOUT US?

In common with all rock 'n' roll acts, The Coasters began to sell fewer and fewer records towards the early sixties. Their decline was synonymous with Leiber and Stoller's increasing involvement with companies other than Atlantic, for whom their productions diminished. By maintaining their independence from Atlantic, Leiber and Stoller had worked for other large companies, particularly Capitol and RCA-Victor, throughout the fifties. Apart from Elvis Presley, they had composed for and/or produced a plethora of middle-of-the-road performers including David Hill, Jack Jones, Julius LaRosa, Perry Como, Steve Lawrence, Ann Leonardo, and Jaye P Morgan. Few records of commercial or artistic importance emerged from these random liaisons but, in 1959, they hooked on to Big Top, a New York independent formed to provide the Hill and Range publishers with a record outlet. Here Leiber and Stoller produced Sammy Turner, Ocie Smith, Gerri Granger, and Azie Mortimer. Turner, a black ex-paratrooper from New Jersey, had one of the most painfully underrated voices to have graced pop music. A sinuous, smoky tenor, each of his enchanting records were stamped with his inimitable, highly stylized approach while the violins, violas, and cellos blended with the stuttering saxophone of King Curtis to produce the most unusual and diverting patterns yet heard in popular music. 'Lavender Blue' (Big Top 3016) made the top three in 1959 while his other records, 'Sweet Annie Laurie' (3007)—searing King Curtis solo here—'Always' (3029), 'Symphony' (3029) and 'Paradise' (3032), notched the popular charts throughout the year. They may not be in everyone's desert island rucksack but collectively,

Turner's records were the pinnacle of symphonic black pop music; short wonder that Phil Spector claims to have produced 'Lavender Blue'.

Leiber and Stoller's work for Big Top and other labels was not, at first, so prolific as to impinge upon their relationship with Atlantic but, by the early sixties, they were heavily involved in negotiating a number of independent production deals with other companies and, concomitantly, their work for Atlantic and Atco became restricted to The Drifters and their breakaway lead singer, Ben E. King. Early in 1961, Leiber and Stoller formed their own company for outside production and began cutting sides for MGM (Roy Hamilton), Capitol (Peggy Lee), Jubilee (Betty Harris), Checker (Dale Hawkins), ABC–Paramount (The Temps), Vee-Jay (Christine Kittrell), Roulette (Myrna March) and, in August of that year, United Artists. In addition to producing these artists, they often wrote the material and handled the arrangements. They were reported to receive two or three cents per side on each disc they produced. 'Cry to Me' (Jubilee 5456) and 'His Kiss' (5465) both powerful numbers for Betty Harris and 'I Keep Forgetting', a song they wrote for Chuck Jackson (Wand 126), deserve a place in any representative collection of early sixties soul. Oddly enough, most of their other excursions were pretty dire. The collaboration with United Artists, though undeniably profitable, was probably the least satisfying of all their new endeavours. Nonetheless, the hits kept on coming including a handful by The Exciters which ought to have been much better than they were. Lush arrangements by the late Teacho Wilshire employed the ethereal strings, marimba, and tom-tom baion beat of earlier Drifters' records while Bert Berns, Van McCoy, and Burt Bacharach supplied a number of potentially soulful songs. But the group were not the best black vocalists ever and it was becoming clear that Leiber and Stoller were inspired only by singers with some degree of emotional tone and colour to their voices. That such a lot of heavy names could crank out records which you would never want to play more than once was surprising to say the least. George Goldner would have made great records with The Exciters: Leiber and Stoller made only boring monuments to their increasing dissaffection with the recording studios. Still, 'Tell Him' (UA 544) was a top ten hit in 1962 and so they carried on. There was Mike Clifford as soppy as a cream puff balladeer; Jay and The Americans, a white and horribly gross version of the Drifters; Steve Lawrence for whom they put words to Debussy's 'My Clair de Lune' (UA 335); even Johnny Ray who had nothing but a deaf-aid going for him in the first place. On Mike Stoller's own admission, all this stuff 'was neither here nor there, we were just doing it!' The money cannot have been important but it was probably better than laying in bed all day. That most of this mediocrity sold records is more distressing than anything else. The Exciters had four big hits while Leiber and Stoller's infinitely superior productions for The Isley Brothers never even dented the Hot Hundred. Even if no one remembers them today, Jay and The Americans still sold almost as many records as The Coasters.

In February 1963, Jerry Leiber attended a NARAS-sponsored New York seminar, 'The Art of Recording', where he gave some insight into the contribution which he and Stoller had made to the industry. The independent producer, he explained, had brought wide diversity and prosperity to a great many musicians, composers, publishers, and artists by breaking up the tightly controlled cliques of talent and material users within major and large independent companies. Eventually, he believed, those indie producers that wanted to grow as a business must have their own labels. Three months before, he and Stoller had, in fact, formed their own label, Tiger, their first since Spark a decade before. One—apparently solitary—release, issued in December 1962, featured a black group, Tippie and The Clovers, singing 'The Bossa Nova (My Heart Said)' and 'Bossa Nova Baby', two somewhat trivial songs which jumped on the band-wagon of the Brazilian dance fad. The record (Tiger 201) was a '*Billboard* Pick of the Week' but neither side was any kind of a hit until October 1963 when Elvis Presley made the top ten with a revival of 'Bossa Nova Baby' (RCA 8243).

In November 1963, Leiber and Stoller formed another label Daisy, and reactivated Tiger as a subsidiary. On this occasion, the *Billboard* despatch reads: 'New York. Leiber and Stoller opened a new diskery here. The new firm will involve two labels, Daisy and Tiger. Leiber and Stoller will continue their indie-producing activities for Jubilee, United Artists, and Atlantic, among others. Involved with the new Leiber and Stoller operation as writers–producers are such teams as Jeff Barry and Ellie Greenwich, David and Bacharach, Van McCoy and Buddy Smith, Norman Rubin will be in charge of sales and promotion.' According to Stoller, 'Daisy was aborted because the first releases came out the day Kennedy was assassinated (22 November 1963).' He described the label as no major loss and he could be right although, of the half-dozen releases, one—'Everybody come Clap your hands' by Moody and The Deltas (Daisy 504)—was attractive. Produced by New Orleans bandleader Joe Jones, the combination of bubblegum teen song and a heavy Southern feel was appealing in a quirky sort of way. The subsidiary company, Tiger—whose releases now began—somewhat confusingly—at 101 with a girl group, The Lovejoys, fared a little better. Records by Bessie Banks, DeeDee Warwick, Alvin Robinson, and Vic Donna followed. Robinson had a hit with 'Something you Got' (104) and 'Go Now' (102), a neurotic slab of neat soul by Bessie Banks, made the British r & b top ten shortly after The Moody Blues had taken a cover version to the top of the pop charts on both sides of The Atlantic in 1965. None of the other releases sold at all and Leiber has explained the problem to Peter Burns of the English magazine, *Cream*: 'We made a few blues records and we couldn't sell them. We didn't know much about merchandising or promoting records and although we'd been in the record business all these years, we'd never had anything to do with the sales department or the promotion department. We'd always been locked in studios or rehearsal rooms. So we went into the record business and part of the whole situation was really our naïvity in manufacturing, sales, and promotion. We knew how to make records but we didn't know how to sell 'em or promote 'em. We made a couple of records we thought were good but nobody played them.'[1]

Two new labels, Red Bird and Blue Cat, were formed to rectify this unfortunate lack of success. Now very much wiser, Leiber and Stoller shared the presidency with George Goldner who had been responsible for hits by Frankie Lymon and The Teenagers and many more black groups during the early years of rock 'n' roll's initial acceptance. In a marvellous interview with Richard Williams of *Melody Maker*, Leiber has explained how he met Goldner by chance in a bar on 54th Street: 'Hymie (Hy Weiss, owner of Old Town) was blowing cigar smoke in George's face. George had lost something in the region of ten or fifteen million dollars at the race track—every great label he'd started, he gambled away. Hymie was baiting George and in his good-natured way George was taking it, and I was having a drink listening to the conversation. They were arguing about the salary that Hy was going to pay George to go to work for Old Town records. George kept insisting ... he was wearing these very elegant clothes but I remember they were a bit frayed ... he was telling Hymie that he couldn't get his shirts done for that kind of money. Hy was saying that he'd have to learn how to live a little more modestly—and at that point I offered George a partnership. Hy thought it was a great joke—I was dead serious. For a moment George couldn't believe it. But I was looking for somebody who could sell, who knew how to merchandise and promote records. We got up and went back to the office. We had about ten or twelve masters, unreleased, and I gave George some acetates. He said, "I'll be back tomorrow morning—I'll stay up all night and listen to them, and if there's a hit in here I'll find it." He was in early the next morning, his eyeballs hanging out of his head and he was very excited and enthusiastic. He held up this one acetate and said, "This is it—I'll bet my life on it." And it was 'Chapel of Love' (Red Bird 10–001), by The Dixie Cups, a record I really hated with a passion."[2]

'Chapel Of Love', written by Phil Spector, Jeff Barry, and Ellie Greenwich topped the pop charts in 1964 selling two million copies on the way. Henceforth, Leiber and Stoller took little interest in the creative end of Red Bird/Blue Cat. They left both song-writing and production to a host of younger talents—Jerry Goffin and Carole King, Barry Mann and Cynthia Weil, Nick Venet, George 'Shadow' Morton, Artie Ripp—and the all-important promotion to George Goldner whose past experience proved invaluable; in terms of '*Billboard*'s Hot Hundred', the complex enjoyed twenty-five hit records in two years. Most were notched up by mixed groups with a female lead, The Jellybeans and The Adlibs, or all girl teams like The Shangri-Las, The Butterflys, and The Dixie Cups. They included, wrote Williams, some of the greatest pop records of all time and deserved to go down in anyone's history of rock 'n' roll. His appreciation can be read in his own book, *Out of His Head; The Sound of Phil Spector*.[3] Bear in mind, however, that the operative word is 'pop' and not 'rock 'n' roll'. Leiber and Stoller would not have confused the terms: 'This whole level and category of songs and recording was out of my ken,' said Leiber. 'I didn't dig it. It was the forerunner of bubblegum music-teenage ballads. Jeff and Ellie wrote most of it. They were like super-aces at making this type of material. Also George Goldner was very much involved with it. That was really the level of music he enjoyed—he hated r & b and didn't understand it.'[4]

Goldner will not have been fascinated by the records of Alvin Robinson, one of the few performers on either label in whom Leiber and Stoller took any interest at all. Born in New Orleans in December 1937, Robinson first played professionally as a guitarist in the band of Joe Jones who became his manager. He recorded for Imperial (1961) and Post (1962) before giving Leiber and Stoller their only hit on Tiger with his revival of the Chris Kenner composition, 'Something you Got'. Arranged by Joe Jones, it was a fine performance, slow and heavy with Robinson's vocal akin to that of his idol, Ray Charles. The reverse, a splendid revival of 'Searchin'' was stark, deep, and fiercely black. But he never made a bad record and the others recorded at the instigation of Leiber and Stoller were among his best. 'I'm gonna put some hurt on you' (Blue Cat 108) with its punchy brass, second line piano, and shouts from the band captures the unmistakable spirit of New Orleans where it was produced and arranged by Joe Jones and Wardell Quezerque in 1965. 'Fever' and the Leiber–Stoller composition, 'Down Home Girl' (Red Bird 10-010), and 'Bottom of my Soul' c & w 'Let The Good Times Roll' (Blue Cat 113), never made the popular lists but Robinson's thick, cracked, and guttural voice was always in fine fettle, and 'Down Home Girl' sparked revivals by The Rolling Stones and The Coasters as well as a sequel by The Adlibs in 'I'm Just a Down Home Girl' (Blue Cat 123). Despite their huge success The Shangri-Las, The Dixie-Cups, The Jellybeans, and The Butterflys evaporated overnight while Robinson, whose talent was as great as theirs was mediocre, continued to record for Joe Jones' own record company, and Atco and Pulsar, well into the early seventies. Leiber and Stoller also produced other Blue Cat artists including The Soul Brothers and Ronnie Mitchell. While Mitchell's brand of good-time r & b does not compare with Robinson's work, he too shines out of the general catalogue like a beacon. Also from New Orleans, he crops up with 'Having a Party' (Blue Cat 111) which, according to the lyric, is attended by Marvin Gaye, Rufus Thomas, and—rather quaint—The Dixie Cups and The Jellybeans. The Beatles were there as well.

It's a fun enough idea and Mike Stoller probably contributes the happy-go-lucky boogie piano.

By 1966, Leiber and Stoller had grown tired of running a record company. Jerry Leiber again: 'We worked hard and it became even more dreary and more demoralizing because I found myself in a living situation that was a big drag. I mean I had to talk to distributors and disc-jockeys and promotors and I wasn't really interested in that kind of a dialogue. I'm not saying that they're a drag. I'm saying that that process, that involvement for me is a drag. I'm not a businessman. I'm a song-writer. It got to a point where we were writing absolutely nothing because the artists on the label didn't interest us in terms of our own efforts and there was no possibility. We couldn't really develop a blues roster because of the nature of the management which was George Goldner. He was interested in pop hits. And so we had less and less to do with the actual writing and production of the records and more and more to do with the administrative end of the business which neither one of us was very well equipped to handle ... So finally we decided to give it up. We gave the business to George and we quit.'[5]

Goldner carried on for a few months but soon began gambling again. To clear his debts he was forced to sell off the Red Bird/Blue Cat masters. Some of the Alvin Robinson material was purchased by Atlantic who have not made it available again. Other cuts began to appear in unlikely places, on Polydor and Shelby Singleton's Nashville-based SSS International label. 'George,' said Stoller, 'sold the exclusive rights on the same tapes to a number of people and we have no rights to them now.'[6] And that was the end of Red Bird. It was not, however, the end of Leiber and Stoller. In fact, they were back with The Coasters before you could say 'Yakety Yak'.

*Billboard* carried news of the reconciliation in March 1967: 'In further artist expansion, Date has made a production agreement with Leiber and Stoller for The Coasters. The group's first single is "Soul Pad" c & w "Down

Home Girl" and an album is now in preparation.' Date was a subsidiary of CBS. It had been formed in 1965 to provide Columbia with 'an additional releasing and promotional outlet for the strong and varied product coming to our attention'. It would, continued the CBS publicity machine, 'quickly establish itself as an important new label.' Sadly perhaps it did nothing of the kind. The carefully promoted aura of mystery and sophistication with which Columbia surrounded its major superstars rarely extended to those acts, usually black, which were tucked away on Date. Leiber and Stoller deserved a better deal but it was not forthcoming as Stoller has explained: 'What was rough about the Columbia deal was that The Coasters didn't have the full support of CBS. They put them on Date and then they said, "Well it's not really r & b and it's not really pop and we're not really strong with the r & b jocks.' I argued of course, I said, "Well first of all The Coasters have never, for the most part, been a really big r & b act." They had colossal r & b hits of course but usually this was a spill-over from the pop market. They always happened pop first and I tried to argue that they really were a pop act but I didn't get anywhere. Let me give you an example. There was one record we made with The Coasters on Date that I thought was really a potential hit. I feel very strongly about it—it was called "DW Washburn". Now CBS said, "We don't think our people can get r & b play on it." I said, "Well it's not an r & b record, y'know what with the banjo an' all." But because of Columbia's attitude it stayed in the can for a while. Then I played the tape to our old partner, Lester Sill, who, at that time, was at Screen-Gems with The Monkees. He said, "Man what a fantastic record", and we said, "Look it doesn't look like they're gonna put the thing out. I mean they just don't seem to know where it's at as far as this kind of production is concerned." Lester said, "Man if they don't do it, I'm gonna grab that song an' I'll do it with The Monkees." We went back to the people at Date and said, "We think we have a big hit here," and they said,

"Well if you want us to put it out, we'll put it out but, y'know, we don't have any faith in it." So I figured it would be better not to have 'em put it out than to have 'em throw it up against the wall and not get any promotion on it. So we let The Monkees have it and, of course, their version became a hit. When they saw what was happening CBS released it by The Coasters. It got good reviews but it was during a CBS convention and it never got played.'

'DW Washburn' was just about as perfect as any pop record could possibly be. A beautifully and carefully constructed scenario of city life it owed much in the way of melodic ideas to the work of The Lovin' Spoonful, particularly their song, 'Daydream' (Kama Sutra 208) a big hit two years before. A wino, played by Billy Guy, hears a voice from the Salvation Army offering a hot bowl of soup, a shave, and some well-intentioned advice.* The vaudeville accompaniment reflects the character's mood; singing through an alcoholic haze he resisted all offers of salvation content to be left alone flat out in the gutter, pie-eyed, befuddled, and happy with only a bottle for company. The version by The Monkees (Colgems 1023) made the top twenty but very few people got to hear The Coasters. That they were ever on Date seems to have been a state secret anyway; an appalling waste for the other records made with Leiber and Stoller during 1967–8 were almost as brilliant as 'DW Washburn' and better than many of their final collaborations on Atlantic during the early sixties. 'Soul Pad' and 'Down Home Girl' was certainly the best double-sider since 1962. The former, a send-up of psychedelic rock, health-food, commune dwellers, half-baked mysticism—indeed all the facets of the alternative society or counter-culture—was as sharp and witty as anything Jerry Leiber had ever composed. Here are two verses:

** I had intended to quote part of the song but was unfortunately unable to arrange satisfactory terms for its inclusion.*

*'Two Russian students hang out in the closet*
*hung up on jazz and funk*
*they keep some incense burning in a sardine can*
*beneath a picture of Thelonius Monk.*

*This FBI agent came to see us*
*said his orders were to check out the freaks*
*he started with a poet in the pantry*
*an' he's been with us now about fourteen weeks.'*

'Down Home Girl', bursting with soul-flecked country blues imagery, was clearly worth reviving. Again, Billy Guy took the suitably lecherous lead vocal and, in addition to the snippet in chapter four, another verse illustrates that Jerry Leiber had retained every inch of his incredible talent for creating powerful and vivid pictures from a mere handful of words:

*'You're sittin' there in that fancy chair*
*drinkin' champagne like a movie star*
*when you oughta be sittin' on a kerbstone*
*sippin' white lightnin' out of a jelly jar.'*

'She Can,' The Coasters final record for Date, was based on 'I'm a Woman' (Capitol 4888) which Leiber and Stoller had written for Peggy Lee in 1962. Lyrically and melodically, the song owed as much to the blues as any of their compositions incorporating at least one traditional fragment of verse which had been used by, among others, Jelly Roll Morton and, in 1939, by Cripple Clarence Lofton who called his composition 'I don't Know'. Mike Stoller however had heard the song by a young Chicago pianist–singer, Willie Mabon, in whose hands a particular metaphor which originally alluded to sexual intercourse while standing up, now referred, more innocently, to a domestic chore:

*'The woman I love she's got dimples on her jaws*
*The clothes she's wearin' is made out of the best of cloth*
*she can take 'em and wash 'em, she can hang 'em upside the wall*
*she can throw 'em out the window an' run out an' catch 'em before they fall'*

In 'She Can', a woman's infinite skills were described over three equally witty verses in much the same way:

*'She can wash out forty pairs of socks an' have 'em hangin' on the line*
*she can starch and iron two dozen shirts fo' you can count from one to nine*
*she can scoop up a great big kipperful of lard from the dripping can*
*throw it in the skillet, go out and shop, be back fo' it melts in the pan.*

*She can rub an' scrub 'til this old house is shining like a Roosevelt dime*
*feed the baby, walk the dog, bake a cherry pie all at the same time*
*she can work all day, party all night, dance 'til 4 o'clock an' then*
*lay down at five, jump up at six and start one more again.*

*She can stretch a greenback dollar bill from here to Kingdom come*
*play the numbers, pay the bills and still end up with some*
*I gotta twenty dollar gold piece that says ain't nothin' she can't do*
*She can make a dress out of a feedbag an' she can make a monkey out of you.'*

The song 'I'm a Woman' recalled Stoller, 'was also influenced by "I'm a Man", y'know the Muddy Waters record. It wasn't conscious oddly enough even though I'm aware of it now. It had to be—The Peggy Lee record was like "She Can" only it had the spelling of W.O.M.A.N. just as Muddy Waters had the spelling of M.A.N. And the kind of phrasing that's involved, especially in the first part of the song, we may have picked that up from Willie Mabon. I remember that I loved his record.' Orchestrally, 'She Can'—arranged by Artie Butler—was a bang up to date, weaving together bass, brass, and an organ solo. It was the only concession to contemporary soul. The Coasters sang as they always had, chopping up the lyric to allow for a variety of lead voices—'Play the Numbers' (Carl Gardner), 'Pay the Bills' (Earl Carroll), 'and still end up with some' (Billy Guy). Artie Butler was also responsible for arranging the flip, 'Everybody's Woman'. A loud, stomping, discotheque record, it is noticeable for the crashing, echoing breaks midway—the antithesis of Leiber and Stoller's normally uncluttered approach but a touch of pure Spector nonetheless.

With the right promotion any one of these sides could have been a smash hit. Columbia's treatment of Leiber and Stoller was inarguably one of the greater tragedies in the history of rock, all the more inexplicable considering the company's pioneering efforts in marketing black music with the Okeh subsidiary. By 1968 however CBS had lost Aretha Franklin to Atlantic and their popular success with black artists was confined very largely to the maudlin duo of Peaches and Herb and the rock-oriented Sly and The Family Stone. They desperately needed more black performers but chose to ignore a ready made opportunity to promote a team whose acceptance would have been assured. Compare, for example, the saga of Kenny Gamble and Leon Huff, song-writing and production collaborators from Philadelphia whose work with Jerry Butler, Wilson Pickett, and Archie Bell and The Drells had made them a force to be reckoned with during the late sixties. In 1971 they assigned distribution rights of their own labels to Columbia. Promptly, and for the first time, photographs of the duo appeared in the trade papers where, all smiles, they posed on either side of Clive Davis, the managing director of Columbia who were now willing to market pop-slanted r & b with a vengeance. Gamble and Huff had made exceptionally good records in that idiom for years without becoming household names; with the might of Columbia's promotion, distribution, and publicity behind them they couldn't fail and, indeed, huge international hits by The O'Jays, Billy Paul, and Harold Melvin and The Bluenotes followed in short order. By 1973 it was impossible to open a rock magazine without reading about Gamble and Huff. What the CBS dinosaur could have achieved behind the world's greatest producers in top form, an institution like The Coasters, and a slew of superb records is difficult to contemplate but clearly all concerned were in the wrong place at the wrong time. Frustrated by the whims and games of businessmen, their masterpieces rendered next to useless by apathetic exposure, Leiber and Stoller terminated their agreement with Columbia and virtually retired from the recording studios for three years.

Left to their own devices, The Coasters signed with Turntable, a small New York independent owned by Lloyd Price and distributed by Jad, an operation owned by Johnny Nash. At Prices Turntable Club on Broadway, they made what is indisputably the worst record of their entire career. Despite a wealth of credits—composed by Jimmy Norman, arranged by Jerry Thomas, produced by Lloyd Price—both sides, 'Act Right' and 'The World is Changing', are cacophonous drivel with no redeeming features. Deservedly, its release passed unnoticed. The name of Jimmy Norman would, however, have excited r & b enthusiasts. A prolific but underrated performer from Los Angeles, Norman had made up to twenty or so records since 1959. After appearing on Mun-rab, Dot, and Raystar, he went to Little Star in 1962 where, produced by H. B. Barnum, he scored a top fifty hit with 'I don't love you no More' (Little Star 113). Unable to consolidate this success, he continued to flit from label to label—Goodsound, Samar, Polo, Mercury—until, in 1973, he joined The Coasters where, like Vernon Harrell before him, he deputized for Billy Guy.

In the meantime, Leiber and Stoller had decided to become business tycoons. If you can't beat them then, join them perhaps. In 1970, in a complex series of negotiations, they began to invest their wealth. With Freddie Bienstock, head of Carlin Music in London, they formed Mirabelle Music in a 50–50 partnership. In one move, the corporation purchased TM Music and other valuable catalogues from Commonwealth United Publishing including the copyright to such durable songs as 'Under The Boardwalk', 'Summer in the City', 'Good lovin' ', and 'Things'. Since leaving Columbia they had entered the recording studios on very few occasions. In 1969, they provided Peggy Lee with a top ten hit, 'Is that all there is' (Capitol 2602), a song which they had extracted from an as yet unproduced Leiber–Stoller musical, 'The International Wrestling Match' and they produced a small hit. 'Do your own Thing', for Brook Benton (Cotillion 44007) the year before. They also scored the sound-track of a Warner Bros. movie, 'The Phynx'; it too has yet to be seen. In October 1971, they surprised the industry by acquiring, with Hal Neely and Fred Bienstock, the world-famous Starday–King label from the Lin Broadcasting Company. A colossal transaction (sale price was listed at almost one and a half million dollars) the assets included thousands of copyrights, publishing interests, recorded masters, inventory, contracts, real estate, recording studios in Nashville, Cincinnati, and Macon as well as a pressing and printing plant in Cincinnati. 'We acquired it,' said Leiber, 'because it already had complete management from top to bottom. We really have nothing to do with the actual day-to-day running of it. It's almost the same situation as working for Atlantic: we go to the studio, master a record, send them the tapes, and that's it.'[7]

If there was a snag, it was the lack of current big-name artists with which to work. Starday, formed as a country label by Pappy Dailey and Jack Starnes, was later acquired by Don Pierce. After the Lin Purchase, Hal Neely became president and, shortly thereafter, many of the leading country performers left the label. King, formed by Syd Nathan, was also a country label originally but became heavily involved in r & b during the early fifties. Prior to the Neely and Leiber–Stoller takeover, King too had divested itself of many of its top performers including James Brown who had moved to Polydor in a contract sale. Now operating under the name of The Tennessee Recording and Publishing Co., Inc., Starday/King and subsidiaries—Deluxe, Nashville, Agape, and Federal—could muster only a handful of successful acts—The Manhattans, Arthur Prysock, Gloria Walker—between them. Not surprisingly, the first tapes which Leiber and Stoller despatched from New York to Nashville included a batch of songs by The Coasters. It was not, however, a preconceived plan. Mike Stoller: 'When the Columbia thing happened we separated, we severed the relationship to everybody's satisfaction. Since then, like ourselves, they hadn't been doing anything very special in the way of records. But we always loved The Coasters, we really did, and after we acquired King, I was walking down the street with Hal Neely and we bumped into the group on Broadway, they were on their way to a weekend gig or something. I said, "Hey come by the office—let's talk." We still had the right to use those sides we had made for CBS including a whole album of material—"Mustang Sally", "Mohair Sam", "Good Lovin'", "On Broadway"—which had never been released. I was particularly fond of one track, "Love Potion No. 9", that we'd done on Date but had never properly finished. We signed The Coasters and went over it again adding a couple of things to it including a flute by a guy named Taco Meza—Taco is a nickname, it's a

Mexican delicacy—he's one of the cats who plays with Tito Puente's band.'

Released in November 1971, 'Love Potion No. 9' made the national top fifty, the top seventy r & b and, in England, the r & b top ten. Originally written for The Clovers whose version (United Artists 180) entered the top thirty in 1959, it is not the wittiest or most ingenious of Leiber–Stoller compositions relying chiefly on an improbable situation which was even less likely to raise a smile twelve years later:

*'I took my troubles down to Madam Ruth*
*y'know that gypsy with the gold cap tooth*
*she's gotta store-front at 34th and Vine*
*serving little bottles of love potion number nine.'*

Lead singer, Carl Gardner, tells Madam Ruth that he's flopped with chicks since 1966 (The Clovers had sung '1956'), obtains a quantity of the magic aphrodisiac and starts kissing everything in sight:

*'... but when I kissed a cop down at 34th and Vine*
*he broke my little bottles of love potion number nine.'*

'Riot in Cell Block No. 9' was a good deal funnier. The production too was in no way recognizably Leiber or Stoller or The Coasters. The flute solo was irritating and the latin arrangement, infectious at first, quickly palled. It was, thought most reviewers, an undistinguished effort from so highly regarded a combination of talents and it smacked of work for old-times sake. No one, it seemed, played the flip-side, a re-issue of the glorious 'DW Washburn', now four years old but unaltered in any way and still sounding perfectly and unmistakably Coasters.

The bass singer on 'Love Potion No. 9' (but not 'DW Washburn') was Ronald Bright, a newcomer to Coasters records who had, nonetheless, been singing with them since

Dub Jones left in 1968 to become, according to various sources, a preacher, a producer, or a restauranteur. England first heard of Bright by name when he wrote to the *Melody Maker* in 1967! As the somewhat virulent letter indicates he had paid his dues in a variety of ways beginning with The Valentines (Richard Barrett, Raymond Briggs, Mickey Francis, Eddy Edgehill, and Bright) in 1955, shortly after the group had enjoyed their first and biggest hit, 'Tonight Kathleen' (Old Town 1009). He stayed with them for their many popular East Coast hits on George Goldner's Rama label including 'Lily Maebelle' (171), 'Woo Woo Train' (196), 'Nature's Creation' (208), and 'Don't say Goodnight' (228) and, in 1959, he sang alongside Earl Carroll in the then declining Cadillacs. The Valentines were one of the innumerable off the street-corner, out of the pool-hall teams in which George Goldner specialized. They made records which Jerry Leiber hates, Jerry Wexler despises and I eat up. Like all Goldner's teenage groups, there's a jaunty lead tenor, a heavy drumbeat, Jimmy Wright's obligatory saxophone solo and breaks in the moronically simple arrangement where the bass singer would offer his glamorous contribution—'oom bah bud doom bah buh doom bah durb durb'. Arriving too late to enjoy any kind of reputation with The Coasters, Bright had been lucky to work consistently in New York City where groups traditionally used a bass as a separate voice well out front and not—like groups from the West Coast—merely another vehicle to add depth to their harmony. When capitalizing on the bass singer went out of style, Bright was able to attract the attention of anyone in the Brill Building who needed a bass voice as a gimmick, a memory of popular music's uncomplicated street heritage. He sang on a number of Jackie Wilson records; put what little glitter there was into Barry Mann's 'Who put the Bomp' (ABC 10237) in 1961 and became 'Mr Bassman' (Kapp 503) on Johnny Cymbal's hit of 1963. Self-consciously clever, the last two records stuck in my throat as the nadir of the New

York group sound. Session work must have been lucrative but dissatisfying and, before joining The Coasters, Bright travelled around the world with The Deep River Boys.

The Coasters' next record, 'Cool Jerk', had been a top ten hit for a black trio The Capitols (Karen 1524) in 1966. Written by a member of the group, Donald Storball, the tune carried an attractive piano figure and had more substance than most dance-craze records although Atlantic's distribution must have assisted its popularity. The Coasters had recorded the song for Columbia in 1967 but it remained on the shelf until issued as a follow-up to 'Love Potion No. 9'. Again, Leiber and Stoller had tinkered with the Columbia tape but, without hearing the original, it's not possible to say quite what improvements were gained. Scarcely any perhaps. It was lively enough but soul fans already had The Capitols record and another version of a six-year-old dance fad, originally intended as an album filler, was not what the world needed most. The reverse, a re-mastered and a re-titled version of 'She Can' called 'Talkin' 'bout a Woman', was hardly more refreshing. Their third King single coupled 'Soul Pad' and—out for the third time—'DW Washburn'. As before it wasn't played. It will probably be issued every two years and Carl Gardner will receive a gold disc when he's eighty.

As well as producing some heavily orchestrated ballads for Arthur Prysock on King, Leiber and Stoller also returned to other company's studios. In 1973 they produced 'Stuck in the Middle with You' (A+M), a world-wide hit for Stealer's Wheel. It was palatable enough, even good of its kind but it didn't sparkle in the way Ben E King used to, and it hadn't got that wit. Nevertheless, Leiber and Stoller were back making records and fresh offers flooded in. They served up a couple of sides by Shark Wilson, a Jamaican singer whose record – 'Too much Pain' c & w 'Where are we going?' (Fresh Air 6121 100)—blended reggae rhythms with Memphis horns and the soulful voices of The Sweet Inspirations. At the time of writing, it does not look as if

Wilson will break Johnny Nash's monopoly over the sophisticated reggae idiom. They also produced a double album on T-Bone Walker (Reprize 2XS 6483) singing some of the blues they had written over twenty years before—'Three Cornpatches', Charles Brown's 'Hard Times', Littlefield's 'Kansas City', 'Striking on you Baby', and others. I've not yet heard it but the project sounds like an interesting and very listenable return to their roots.

As far as their own company was concerned, Leiber and Stoller seemed to have lost the Midas touch and, once again, the games of businessmen weighed against The Coasters career. In October 1973, *Billboard* reported a disagreement between the principals of Starday–King. Leiber, Stoller, and Bienstock, who owned 70 per cent of the shares, had voted out president Hal Neely who retained 30 per cent. Each party had tried to buy out the other's interest and failed to find a compromise. The disagreement arose, said Neely, because Starday–King had not had a hit record for nine months; the sale of the label to a third party was contemplated. Later the same month, Bienstock replaced Neely as president and announced plans for expansion. A progressive label, Good Medicine, was said to have been formed. But, on 1 December, *Billboard* revealed that Starday–King had ceased operations and that the entire complex was up for sale again. To date, the matter remains unresolved and quite where this leaves The Coasters no one knows. A year before, Billy Guy had been reasonably optimistic about the groups' future, hit records or not.

' "Love Potion No. 9" may be the first record we've had in so long but we do three, four, or five nights a week, every week. We've never stopped working, never have. What other group can you say that about? Name one that's been going twenty years. I only know of us and The Dells but they had to make a comeback, they had broken up and had to get together again. The dancing groups like The Cadillacs killed their ownselves and many of the bird groups never sold more than 200,000 copies. There were new groups coming up everyday in the r & b field but they were as good as their last record and they couldn't make the top twenty at first. To do that you had to lie—you had to sing, "Darling I'll swim the mountains", y'know, "An I'll climb the sea". You couldn't come out and sing "Baby I love you an' that's that". I was so glad when white kids began buying honest music. That's why we've survived. Our first records went *per se* 80 per cent white. We were the first black group to go pop and build on that, we were the first black group to break comedy as a considered rock 'n' roll act. There isn't another group like us, no one's gonna jump on us, no one else even attempted it. Whatever we've been doing, we've already tried it every feasible way before we recorded it. If you wanna hear "Searchin' ", "Yakety Yak" or "Charlie Brown", you gotta have The Coasters. I think that's really kept us alive, I can see us playing the same clubs for the rest of our lives.'

The Coasters may potter about on various small labels for another five or ten years. They may never be out of work but without records that sell, they are clearly destined to become a rock 'n' roll museum piece. Of four sides for King, all had been wholly or partially recorded for Columbia, two having been hits for other groups. They were not necessarily bad revivals. The question which puzzled most Coasters' fans was why they should need to lean quite so heavily on previous triumphs, their own or someone else's. That Leiber and Stoller had moved on to fresh and, for them, more exciting ways in which to divest their creative energies was the sad but inescapable conclusion. It was nice to have The Coasters back sure but producing another 'Idol with The Golden Head' . . . well it was too long ago. Better to tinker about with some filler tracks from an unreleased album and issue those. Whatever Leiber and Stoller do next could be an extension of The Coasters but not a recession. Rock is heavy, camp, arty, or boring. It isn't funny any more. Rock lost its sense of humour when Stan Freberg went back to advertising, when The Big Bopper fell out of the sky and when 'Little Egypt' slipped down the 'Hot Hundred'.

So, a rock 'n' roll museum piece ... ultimately I can think of nothing more worthy of preservation. Think about it and remember—if you can listen to the radio and still crack a smile, they just have to be playing a Coasters record.

## WHERE ARE THEY NOW?

### THE CAST IN ORDER OF APPEARANCE

TY TERRELL. When the Robins broke up, Terrell remained on the West Coast where he recorded with Little Caesar (real name Carl Burnett) and by himself (e.g. 'The Scratch', parts 1 and 2—Lute 5802). 'I haven't,' recalled Otis, 'seen Roy or Billy in recent years but I've seen Ty. He does something at the airport, he has a private limousine, and he's very youthful and has a lot of energy. I was pleasantly surprised to see him in such good spirits.'

BILLY RICHARDS. Richards lives in Los Angeles but is no longer active in music. A nephew, Billy Richards Junior, now sings with Bobby Nunn's breakaway Coasters.

ROY RICHARDS. Roy Richards also lives in L.A. but was said to be seriously ill in September 1973.

JOHNNY OTIS. Otis went on to provide the springboard for the careers of many r & b singers (Little Willie John, The Midnighters, Etta James) and by 1958 he was writing and arranging rock 'n' roll to order. 'Ma he's making eyes at me' (Capitol 3800), with a vocal by Marie Adams, topped the British charts and Otis enjoyed a string of crisp, clean, and snappy hits for the same label under his own name. Rock 'n' roll novelties didn't come any better than 'Bye Bye Baby' (3852), 'Willie and The Handjive' (3966) and 'Mumblin Mosie' (4326). In 1960, his own label, Eldo, gave us hits by The Safaris and H. B. Barnum. In 1963, by which time he had played or sung on over *600* records, Otis retired to his chicken ranch. In 1967 he re-emerged and recorded blues for Kent and Epic; albums for both labels met with overwhelming critical acclaim. Publication of the definitive Otis biography, by Norbert Hess, is keenly awaited; it will contain further interviews with The Robins, Ralph Bass, Big Jay McNeely, and others.

BOBBY NUNN. Nunn, who believes that he left The Coasters before Leon Hughes, also told Dick Horlick that he was advised to retire on health grounds. On recovery, he formed his own group of Coasters with Billy Wilson, Bobby Sheen (of Bob B. Soxx and Blue Jeans fame) and Grady Chapman. He also worked as a session singer ('my name's on every studio wall in L.A.') backing up country star Dorsey Burnette among others. He now runs a fake Coasters Mark II with Grady Chapman, Billy Richards Jnr. and Randy Jones. Nunn still carries a sleeve of the first Coasters album around with him and has no trouble convincing club-owners that he, at least, is an original.

JOHNNY MOORE. The father of the cool, late-night, cocktail blues sound, Moore died in L.A. of a kidney infection in 1968. He was 62 years old.

HERMAN LUBINSKY. The owner of Savoy, Lubinsky had a heart attack in October 1973. Almost 80 years old, he is currently recuperating in Newark, New Jersey.

RALPH BASS. Before he left Federal, Bass had brought both the Dominoes and James Brown to the label. Around 1960, he went to Chess where he still produces most of the label's blues acts and refuses to work with anything more complicated than four-track.

PETE LEWIS. Lewis, whose distinctive guitar enhanced the work of Little Willie Littlefield, Mama Thornton, Little

Richard, and Johnny Ace, made his own blues instrumentals for Federal and Peacock in 1952 but was unable to find much work after '55. 'Pete died last year' (1971), said Otis. 'Unfortunately he had degenerated into a complete alcoholic.'

MARIO DE LA GARDE. Delagarde, Otis bass-player and tutor to the Robins, was 'very, very political'. He joined the Cuban revolution and perished in the fighting.

LITTLE ESTHER. After making 'Release Me' on Lenox, Esther Phillips recorded for Atlantic and Roulette. An erratic hit-maker throughout the sixties, she is now reaching a sophisticated audience with jazz-blues albums on Kudu.

BIG JOHN DOLPHIN. In 1954, Dolphin's label, Recorded in Hollywood, was bought by Don Pierce who moved it to Nashville as a subsidiary of Starday. Dolphin was shot to death in his L.A. office during the early sixties.

MAGGIE HATHAWAY. A prominent civil rights worker during the sixties, Maggie is now a golfer of some repute.

LESTER SILL. Currently the boss of Screen-Gems, Sill helped manufacture The Monkees and The Archies during the late sixties. Following a recent heart attack he's eased up a little. 'He was as good as any manager around,' said Carl Gardner, 'I reckon if I was managing people I might screw a little on the side as well.'

GRADY CHAPMAN. After leaving The Robins, Chapman sang with The Suedes on Money and, from 1956 to 1961, made a pile of records under his own name. Here's a list: 'I need you so'/'Don't Blooper' (Money 204); 'Say you will be mine'/'Starlight starbright' (Knight 2003); 'Tell me that you care'/'Garden of Memories' (Imperial 5591);

'Let's talk about us'/'Come Away' (Imperial 5611); 'My Love will never change'/'Smiling Gondolier' (Zephyr 70–016); 'Sweet Thing'/'I know what I want' (Mercury 71632); 'Roly Poly' (Arwin). He now sings with Bobby Nunn's Coasters.

GIL BERNAL. Bernal also recorded for American and RCA-Victor. Otis saw him performing in L.A. in 1968: 'A great, swinging, rocking player.'

RICHARD BERRY. Johnny Otis again: 'Richard has carved a corner for himself in L.A. where he has a tremendous following of white kids mostly. He has his own thing, a r & b, rock, pop combination. He plays electric piano and he's gotta guy on congas, a tenor man, and a drummer and he hypnotizes the crowd with a real funky groove.' Berry has also recorded for Bold Soul ('Something'/'Frito Bandito' (Bold Soul 1001)) and, more recently, with rockabilly Ray Campi, for 'Rollin' Rock', owned by Ron Weiser whose records may be obtained from 10735 Bluffside Drive, North Hollywood, California 91604.

H. B. BARNUM. Barnum became a solo performer with records on Fidelity, Munrab, Eldo (he hit the top 40 with 'Lost Love', Eldo 111, in 1961), Imperial, and RCA before developing into a black-jack of all trades. He led a 30-piece band behind rock 'n' roll shows at Cow Palace; owned several small labels Little Star, Prelude, Three) and scored music for TV commercials. By the late sixties, he was earning 50,000 dollars a year as an arranger with RCA, Sue, Capitol (Lou Rawls in particular), and Imperial.

LEON HUGHES. Reported to have sung with The Lamplighters and The Four Flames but confirmation was never forthcoming. Probably back in the car-wash.

Adolph Jacobs. The first Coasters guitarist, Jacobs previously played with Vernon Green and The Medallions. He also made one record for Class ('Walkin' and Whistlin'', 253) in September 1959 and still lives in L.A. where he was recently produced by Kent Harris on material which has not been issued to date.

Young Jessie. A prolific—many records on Atco, Atlantic, Capitol, Mercury, Vanessa, Bit—but hugely underrated artist, Jessie struggles from label to label without a hit. 1972 saw him recording as Obe Jessie and The Seeds of Freedom for a L.A. company, Stone Dogg.

Bob London. London had two more records ('I sailed the seven seas'/'Lovewords', Vita 118 and 'The Cathedral of Notre Dame'/'Catalogue of Love', Dore 596) and then ... nothing.

Cornel Gunter. Gunter still leads a 'fake' Coasters who now (September 1973) include Teddy Harper and Nathaniel Wilson.

Will 'Dub' Jones. Whereabouts of Jones are a mystery but he is believed to have recorded as part of a duo, Cora and Dub, for Atlantic in the late sixties.

The Flairs. In 1961, The Flairs changed their name to The Flares and had a well deserved hit with 'Footstompin'' (Felsted 8624). The group (Aaron Collins, Willie Davis, George Hollis, and Thomas Miller) enjoyed several other popular records on Press and, following on from Cornel Gunter's sister, Shirley Gunter, picked up a succession of female singers including Beverley Harris, Patience Valentine, and Cookie Jackson. They subsequently changed their name to The Redwoods (on Epic) but finally disintegrated around 1964.

King Curtis. Curtis made the top twenty in 1962 with 'Soul Twist' (Enjoy 1000). Nothing else recorded under his own name was as big as that but later records on Capitol and Atco also made the charts. In the late sixties his soul saxophone playing became an indispensable part of records by Aretha Franklin, Donny Hathaway, and other Atlantic artists. On the verge of vastly increased recognition, Curtis was stabbed to death in Harlem on 13 August 1971.

Sonny Forriest. Forriest cut a number of singles (Atco, Verve, Escort, Red Top) around New York. In 1962 he joined the Ray Charles orchestra and subsequently moved into jazz with an album, 'Tuff Pickin'', on Decca (DL 4716).

Kent Harris. Harris moved into production in 1961 scoring with instrumental hits for The Duals ('Stick Shift', Sue 745) and Hank Jacobs ('So Far Away', Sue 795). More recently, he owned a blues label, Romark, and cut sides by Jimmy Ellis, Mighty Hannibal, and Adolph Jacobs. Also owns the Target record shop in L.A.

Lee Hazlewood. An inventive producer, Hazlewood put Nancy Sinatra in the charts ('These Boots are made for walking', Reprise 0432) in 1966. During 1970 he ventured into film acting and now makes television variety programmes in Sweden where he lives for much of the year.

Dallas Frazier. Frazier made it big. Following 'There goes my Everything' in 1967, over fifty of his compositions made the C & W charts and he's now one of the richest composers in country music.

VERNON HARRELL. Harrell never recorded with The Coasters but made a great many solo records including material on Lescay (1962), Decca, Score (1966), U.A., and Brunswick (1971).

CARL GARDNER, BILLY GUY (or JIMMY NORMAN), EARL CARROLL, and RONALD BRIGHT are still (September 1973) performing as THE COASTERS.

# JERRY LEIBER–MIKE STOLLER COMPOSITIONS

## 1951–1970

| *Original Recording Artist* | *Title and Co-Writers* | *Label* | *Year* |
|---|---|---|---|
| RAY AGEE | Another Fool | Spark 119 | 1954/5 |
| PATTY ANDREWS* | Broken | Capitol 3495 | 1956? |
| LAVERN BAKER | Whipper Snapper | Atlantic 1189 | 1958 |
| | Don Juan | ,, 2099 | 1961 |
| | Saved | ,, 2099 | ,, |
| LAVERN BAKER AND JIMMY RICKS | You're The Boss | Atlantic 2090 | 1961 |
| RICHIE BARRETT | Some Other Guy (+ Barrett) | Atlantic 2142 | 1962 |
| | Tricky Dicky | ,, 2142 | ,, |
| GIL BERNAL | Easyville (+ Bernal) | Spark 102 | 1954 |
| | Strawberry Stomp (+ Bernal) | ,, 106 | ,, |
| | King Solomon's Blues (+ Bernal) | ,, 106 | ,, |
| | The Whip (+ Bernal) | ,, 102 | ,, |
| CHARLES BROWN | Hard Times | Aladdin 3218 | 1952 |
| RUTH BROWN | I want to do more | Atlantic 1082 | 1956 |
| | I still love you | ,, 1113 | ,, |
| | Lucky Lips | ,, 1125 | 1957 |
| | Jack O'Diamonds | ,, 2026 | 1959 |
| | I Can't Hear a Word You Say | ,, 2026 | ,, |
| | Papa Daddy | ,, 2035 | ,, |
| | Here he comes (+ Rosemary McCoy & Luther Dixon) | ,, 2088 | 1961 |
| SOLOMON BURKE | You Can't Love 'em all (+ Ertegun & Russell) | Atlantic LP 8096 | 1963 |
| BOYS IN THE BAND | The Boys in the Band | Spring 103 | 1970 |
| LEONARD CARBO | I'll never let you go (+ Carbo) | Atlantic unissued | |
| THE CHEERS | Blueberries | Capitol 3075 | 1954 |
| | Can't we be more than Friends | ,, 3075 | ,, |
| | Fancy meeting you here | ,, 3146 | 1955 |
| | Black Denim Trousers | ,, 3219 | ,, |
| | Chicken (+ Jack Rollins) | ,, 3353 | ,, |
| | Bazoom | ,, | ,, |
| | Que Pasa Muchacha | ,, 3409 | ,, |
| MIKE CLIFFORD | Just Another Girl | U.A. 489 | 1962 |
| PERRY COMO | Dancin' | RCA-Victor 6991 | 1957 |
| CHRIS CONNOR | I only want some | Atlantic 2053 | 1960 |
| CLOVERS | Love Potion No. 9 | U.A. 180 | 1959 |
| | Stay Awhile | ,, 180 | ,, |
| | Lovey | ,, 209 | 1960 |
| COASTERS | Down in Mexico | Atco 6064 | 1956 |
| | One Kiss Led to Another | ,, 6073 | ,, |
| | Turtle Dovin' | ,, 6064 | ,, |
| | Young Blood (+ Doc Pomus) | ,, 6087 | 1957 |
| | Searchin' | ,, 6087 | ,, |
| | My Baby Comes to Me | ,, 6098 | ,, |
| | Idol with The Golden Head | ,, 6098 | ,, |

| *Original Recording Artist* | *Title and Co-Writers* | *Label* | *Year* |
|---|---|---|---|
| | What is The Secret of Your Success | ,, 6104 | ,, |
| | Dance | ,, 6111 | ,, |
| | Gee Golly | ,, 6111 | ,, |
| | Three Cool Cats | ,, 6132 | 1958 |
| | Yakety Yak | ,, 6116 | ,, |
| | Stewball | ,, 6168 | ,, |
| | The Shadow Knows | ,, 6126 | ,, |
| | Sorry But I'm gonna Have to Pass | ,, 6126 | ,, |
| | Charlie Brown | ,, 6132 | ,, |
| | I'm a Hog for You | ,, 6146 | ,, |
| | Along Came Jones | ,, 6141 | 1959 |
| | That is Rock 'n' Roll | ,, 6141 | ,, |
| | What About Us | ,, 6153 | ,, |
| | Poison Ivy | ,, 6146 | ,, |
| | Run Red Run | ,, 6153 | ,, |
| | Lady-Like | ,, 6341 | ,, |
| | Thumbin' A Ride | ,, 6186 | 1960 |
| | Dogface | Unissued | ,, |
| | Keep on Rollin' | Atco 6192 | ,, |
| | Girls Girls Girls | ,, 6204 | 1961 |
| | Little Egypt | ,, 6192 | ,, |
| | Hungry | ,, 6341 | ,, |
| | Bad Blood | ,, 6210 | ,, |
| | The Climb | ,, 6234 | 1962 |
| | Bull Tick Waltz | ,, 6251 | ,, |
| | Down Home Girl | Date 1552 | 1967 |
| | Soul Pad | ,, 1552 | ,, |
| | She Can a.k.a. Talkin'bout a Woman | ,, 1607 | ,, |
| | Everybody's Woman | ,, 1607 | ,, |
| | D W Washburn | ,, 1617 | ,, |
| CRESCENDOS | Sweet Dreams | Atlantic 1109 | 1956 |
| | Finders Keepers | ,, 1109 | ,, |
| CUES* | Charlie Brown | Capitol 3310 | 1956 |
| KING CURTIS | Heavenly Blues | Atco 6152 | 1959 |
| VIC DAMONE* | The Wind Song | Mercury 70480 | 1957? |
| FLOYD DIXON | Too Much Jelly Roll | Aladdin 3111 | 1951 |
| LONNIE DONEGAN | Lorelei | Atlantic 2081 | 1961 |
| DRIFTERS | Ruby Baby | Atlantic 1089 | 1955 |
| | Fools Fall in love | ,, 1123 | 1956 |
| | Drip Drop | ,, 1187 | 1958 |
| | Dance with Me (+ Nathan & Treadwell) | ,, 2040 | 1959 |
| | Rat Race (+ Van McCoy) | ,, 2191 | 1963 |
| | If You don't Come Back | ,, 2191 | ,, |
| | On Broadway (+ Weil & Mann) | ,, 2182 | ,, |
| | Only in America (+ Weil & Mann) | ,, LP 40412 | ,, |
| EXCITERS | Get Him (+ Bert Berns & Passman) | U.A. 604 | 1963 |
| LARRY EVANS | What About Me | Fabor 4009 | 1956? |
| GARLAND THE GREAT | Three Stump Jump | Spark 121 | 1955 |
| | Hello Miss Sims (+ Emanuel) | ,, 121 | ,, |
| | Strike a Match | Atlantic unissued | 1956 |
| BIG JOHN GREER | Drinkin' Fool | RCA-Victor 20-5531 | 1953 |
| BETTY HARRIS | His Kiss (Stoller & Bert Russell only) | Jubilee 5465 | 1964 |
| ROY HAMILTON | You Still Love Him (+ Van McCoy) | MGM 13138 | 1963 |

| *Original Recording Artist* | *Title and Co-Writers* | *Label* | *Year* |
|---|---|---|---|
| PETER HANLEY* | I wanna See You When You Weep | Verve 10028 | |
| WYNONIE HARRIS | Destination Love | Atco 6081 | 1956 |
| SCREAMIN' JAY HAWKINS | Alligator Wine | Okeh 7101 | 1957 |
| DAVID HILL | Cha! Bull! (The Crowd) | RCA-Victor 47-7322 | 1959? |
| LINDA HOPKINS | Get off My Wagon | Crystalette | |
| | Is This Goodbye | ,, | |
| | Two Time Loser | ,, | |
| | Tears of Joy | ,, | |
| HONEY-BEARS | I shall not Fail | Spark 111 | 1954 |
| | It's a Miracle | ,, 104 | ,, |
| | One Bad Stud | ,, 104 | ,, |
| | Whoa! (Bunghole) | ,, 111 | ,, |
| ISLEY BROTHERS | Teach me how to Shimmy | Atlantic 2092 | 1960 |
| | Write to Me (+ Sally Isley) | ,, 2110 | 1961 |
| | Your Old Lady (+ Isley & Curtis) | ,, 2110 | ,, |
| | You'll Never Leave Him (Stoller & Berns only) | U.A. 659 | 1963 |
| CHUCK JACKSON | I keep Forgettin' | Wand 126 | 1962 |
| DAMITA JO | I'll be There (+ Ben E. King & Ollie Jones) | Mercury 71840 | 1961 |
| JACK JONES | You Laugh | Capitol 3991 | 1959? |
| BEN E. KING | Spanish Harlem (Leiber & Phil Spector only) | Atco 6185 | 1960 |
| | On The Horizon | ,, 6194 | 1961 |
| | Yes | ,, LP 142 | 1962 |
| | Stand By Me (+ Ben E. King) | ,, 6194 | 1960 |
| | I Who Have Nothing (+ Donida & Mogul) | ,, 6267 | 1963 |
| | Gypsy (+ Ertegun & Russell) | ,, 6275 | ,, |
| | Where's The Girl | ,, 6596 | 1966 |
| LITTLE ESTHER | Mainliner | Federal 12100 | 1952 |
| | Street Lights | ,, 12122 | ,, |
| | Flesh Blood and Bones | ,, 12108 | ,, |
| | Hollerin' and Screamin' | ,, 12115 | ,, |
| LITTLE ESTHER AND BOBBY NUNN | Saturday Night Daddy | Federal 12100 | 1952 |
| | You Took My Love Too Fast (Stoller & Darnell only) | ,, 12122 | ,, |
| LITTLE ESTHER AND LITTLE WILLIE LITTLEFIELD | Last Laugh Blues | Federal 12108 | 1952 |
| | Turn The Lamps Down Low | ,, 12115 | ,, |
| JULIUS LAROSA | Famous Last Words | RCA-Victor 47-6988 | 1958? |
| STEVE LAWRENCE | My Clair de Lune (+ Debussy) | U.A. 335 | 1961 |
| ANN LEONARDO* | Three Time Loser | Capitol 3817 | 1959? |
| PEGGY LEE | I'm a Woman | Capitol 4888 | 1963 |
| | Is That All There Is | ,, 2602 | 1969 |
| | Whistle for Happiness | ,, LP 21543 | ,, |
| LITTLE WILLIE LITTLEFIELD | K.C. Lovin' a.k.a. Kansas City | Federal 12110 | 1952 |
| | Strikin' on You Baby | ,, 12101 | ,, |
| | Blood is Redder Than Wine | ,, 12101 | ,, |
| | Pleading at Midnight | ,, 12110 | ,, |
| BOB LONDON | Lola | Spark 109 | 1954 |
| | Reckless | ,, 109 | ,, |
| PRESTON LOVE Orch. (vocal by BEVERLY WRIGHT | Kissin' Boogie | Spin 102 | 1952? |
| | Feel so Good (+ Otis) | ,, 103 | |
| JOHNNY MATHIS* | All is Well | Columbia 41583 | |
| FRANKIE MARSHALL | Fanny Lou | Atco 6070 | 1956 |

| *Original Recording Artist* | *Title and Co-Writers* | *Label* | *Year* |
|---|---|---|---|
| | Why Oh Why (Marshall) | ,, 6070 | ,, |
| | Just Say The Word | Spark 117 | 1955 |
| | If it's the last Thing I Do | Atco 6061 | 1956 |
| | Song from My Heart | ,, 6061 | ,, |
| | Every Minute of The Day | ,, 6076 | ,, |
| | Over and Over | ,, 6076 | ,, |
| CLYDE MCPHATTER | You'll be There (+ Relf) | Atlantic 1158 | 1957 |
| JAYE P. MORGAN | My Blind Date | RCA-Victor 47-7178 | 1957? |
| | Tell Me More | RCA-Victor 47-7178 | ,, |
| BETTY JEAN MORRIS | Shack Daddy | Capitol 3296 | 1955 |
| | I Ain't Gonna Mambo | ,, 3296 | |
| AMOS MILBURN | Good Good Whiskey* | Aladdin 3218 | 1952 |
| | Flying Home (+ Goodman & Hampton) | ,, 3125 | ,, |
| AZIE MORTIMER | Lips | Big Top | 1960 |
| OLYMPICS | Loop de Loop Limbo | Tri-Disc LP 1001 | 1963 |
| ELVIS PRESLEY | Hot Dog | RCA-Victor LP 1515 | 1957 |
| | Loving You | 7000 | ,, |
| | Jailhouse Rock | 7035 | ,, |
| | Treat Me Nice | 7035 | ,, |
| | I Want to be Free | EP 4114 | |
| | Baby I don't Care | EP 4114 | |
| | Don't | 7150 | 1958 |
| | Santa Claus is Back in Town | LP 1035 | ,, |
| | Steadfast, Loyal and True | LP 1884 | ,, |
| | King Creole | LP 1884 | ,, |
| | Trouble | LP 1884 | ,, |
| | Dirty Dirty Feeling | LP 2231 | 1960 |
| | She's Not You (+ Pomus) | 8041 | 1962 |
| | Just Tell Her Jim Said Hello | 8041 | ,, |
| | Live it Up | Unissued | |
| | Without You | ,, | |
| | Sands of Time | ,, | |
| | Yeah Yeah Yeah | ,, | |
| | You can't blame a Guy for Trying | ,, | |
| | Bourbon Street | ,, | |
| MISTER RUFFIN | A Touch of Heaven | Spark 115 | 1954 |
| | Bring it on Back | ,, 115 | |
| ROBINS | That's what The Good Book Says | Modern 807 | 1951 |
| | Ten Days in Jail | RCA-Victor 5489 | 1953 |
| | The Hatchet Man | Spark 116 | 1954/55 |
| | One Kiss | ,, 113 | ,, |
| | Wrap it up | ,, 103 | ,, |
| | Riot in Cell Block No. 9 | ,, 103 | ,, |
| | Just Like A Fool | ,, 122 | ,, |
| | Loop de Loop Mambo | ,, 107 | ,, |
| | I Must Be Dreamin' | ,, 116 | ,, |
| | Framed | ,, 107 | ,, |
| | Smokey Joe's Cafe | ,, 122 | ,, |
| | Whadaya Want | ,, 110 | ,, |
| | If Teardrops were Kisses | ,, 110 | ,, |
| TOMMY SANDS* | That's The Way I Am | Capitol 4259 | 1960? |
| OCIE SMITH | Well I'm Dancin' | Big Top 3039 | 1960 |
| WILLIE MAE THORNTON | Hound Dog | Peacock 1612 | 1952 |
| | Nightmare (+ Johnny Otis) | ,, 1612 | ,, |
| | I Smell a Rat | Peacock 1632 | 1952 |
| TIPPY AND CLOVERS | Bossa Nova Baby | Tiger 201 | 1962 |

| *Original Recording Artist* | *Title and Co-Writers* | *Label* | *Year* |
|---|---|---|---|
| | My Heart Said (+ Mann & Weil) | „ 201 | „ |
| JOE TURNER | The Chicken and The Hawk | Atlantic 1080 | 1955 |
| SAMMY TURNER | Falling | Big Top 3089 | 1960 |
| MILT TRENIER and his solid six | You're Killing Me | RCA-Victor 5487 | 1953 |
| | Flip Our Wigs | „ 5487 | „ |
| JUNE VALLI | Will You Love Me Still | RCA-Victor 6852 | 1956? |
| WILLIE and RUTH | Come a Little Bit Closer | Spark 101 | 1954 |
| | Farewell, Farewell | „ 101 | „ |
| | Love Me | „ 105 | „ |
| | Cordelia | „ 105 | „ |
| JIMMY WITHERSPOON | Real Ugly Woman | Modern 821 | 1951 |
| | Corn Whiskey* | Federal 12107 | 1952 |
| MEL WALKER with JOHNNY OTIS ORCH. | Candle's Burning Low | Mercury 8295 | 1952 |
| YOUNG JESSIE | Here Comes Henry (+ George Motola) | Modern 1010 | 1956 |

*Note 1:* * = Conjectural assumption.

*Note 2:* Leiber and Stoller have also claimed to have written songs for Billy Eckstine, Eddie Fisher, Peppermint Harris, Roy Hawkins, Helen Humes, Bullmoose Jackson, Billy May, Lucky Millinder, and Lloyd Price.

*Note 3:* The following forty-one songs are registered with the Aberbach Group of Music Publishing Companies as being Leiber–Stoller compositions. The *original* recording artist is not known to the author but some selections may well be unrecorded or unissued.

A Message from Garcia
Beautiful
Beware
Blues For Me
Cafe Espresso
California Christmas
C'est La Vie
Cool Sweet Boogie
Don't Want No Women
El Tigre
Faye's Boogie
Footsteps
Hangman's Tree
Happy Little Snapdragon
Haven't We Met Before
How Can You do this to Me
I Cry
If I Should Cry
I'll be Right on Down
I'm Only Human
It's been so Long
Let's be Sweethearts Again
Live and Learn
Love Livin' Lover
Love Me, Love Me
Old Fashioned
Ooh Hot Dog (Leiber–Davenport only
Open Fire
Philadelphia Mambo
Please don't Stop
Red Roses
Squeeze Me
That's Life
The Draw
There's a River
Think of Me
Three Corn Patches (recently recorded by Elvis Presley & T-Bone Walker)
Three Thousand Miles from Nowhere
Unconditionally Yours
When The Dance is Over
When You're Young and in Love

THE ROBINS' AND THE COASTERS'

| | Title | Label and number |
|---|---|---|
| ROBINS | If it's so Baby | Savoy 726 |
| ,, | Double Crossin' Blues | Savoy 731 |
| ,, | Smokey Joe's Cafe | Atco 6059 |
| COASTERS | Down in Mexico | Atco 6064 |
| ,, | One kiss led to another | Atco 6073 |
| ,, | Young Blood | Atco 6087 |
| ,, | Searchin' | Atco 6087 |
| ,, | Idol with the Golden Head | Atco 6098 |
| ,, | Yakety Yak | Atco 6116 |
| ,, | Charlie Brown | Atco 6132 |
| ,, | Along came Jones | Atco 6141 |
| ,, | Poison Ivy | Atco 6146 |
| ,, | I'm a hog for you | Atco 6146 |
| ,, | What about Us | Atco 6153 |
| ,, | Run Red Run | Atco 6153 |
| ,, | Besame Mucho | Atco 6163 |
| ,, | Wake me Shake Me | Atco 6168 |
| ,, | Shoppin' for Clothes | Atco 6178 |
| ,, | Wait a Minute | Atco 6186 |
| ,, | Little Egypt | Atco 6192 |
| ,, | Girls Girls Girls | Atco 6204 |
| ,, | T'aint Nothin' to Me | Atco 6287 |
| ,, | Love Potion No 9 | King 6385 |
| ,, | Cool Jerk | King 6389 |

Acknowledgements to *Billboard*, *Record Research* and* *Blues and Soul*.

| HOT 100 | | | R & B CHART | | |
|---|---|---|---|---|---|
| *Date of entry* | *Position reached* | *Weeks on chart* | *Date of entry* | *Position reached* | *Weeks on chart* |
| — | — | — | 27/1/50 | 14 | 1 |
| — | — | — | 27/1/50 | 1 | 22 |
| 23/11/55 | 79 | 1 | 23/11/55 | 13 | 2 |
| — | — | — | 21/3/56 | 9 | 6 |
| 12/9/56 | 73 | 1 | — | — | — |
| 1/5/57 | 8 | 24 | 15/5/57 | 1 | 18 |
| 8/5/57 | 5 | 26 | | | |
| 12/10/57 | 64 | 6 | — | — | — |
| 24/5/58 | 1 | 16 | 31/5/58 | 1 | 14 |
| 8/2/59 | 2 | 15 | 22/2/59 | 2 | 12 |
| 24/5/59 | 9 | 12 | 14/7/59 | 14 | 6 |
| 30/8/59 | 7 | 16 | 7/9/59 | 1 | 16 |
| 13/9/59 | 38 | 8 | — | — | — |
| 13/12/59 | 47 | 10 | 17/1/60 | 17 | 6 |
| 27/12/59 | 36 | 8 | 20/12/59 | 29 | 1 |
| 8/5/60 | 70 | 3 | — | — | — |
| 26/6/60 | 51 | 9 | 30/7/60 | 14 | 8 |
| 9/10/60 | 83 | 4 | — | — | — |
| 5/2/61 | 37 | 8 | — | — | — |
| 30/4/61 | 23 | 12 | 18/6/61 | 16 | 4 |
| 20/8/61 | 96 | 2 | — | — | — |
| 28/3/64 | 64 | 6 | — | — | — |
| | | | 3/12/71 | 65 | 4* |
| | | | 28/4/72 | 95 | 1* |

## DISCOGRAPHY

| | | | |
|---|---|---|---|
| arr | arranger | Lon | London |
| as | alto saxophone | orch | orchestra |
| Atl | Atlantic | org | organ |
| b | bass | Par | Parlophone |
| bgo | bongo | perc | percussion |
| bjo | banjo | p | piano |
| bs | baritone saxophone | SS | Stateside |
| CBS | Columbia | tb | trombone |
| dm | drums | tp | trumpet |
| dir | directed | ts | tenor saxophone |
| f-b | fender-bass | vbs | vibes |
| g | guitar | vo | vocal |
| hca | harmonica | ( ) | unknown instrument |

Numbers in parentheses after a song-title are re-allocated matrix numbers.

BB, CB, and RW followed by a date, in parentheses after a song-title, refers to the *Billboard*, *Cashbox*, or *Record World* review of that recording.

Excelsior 500s, California 300s, Score 4000s, Aladdin 3000s, Savoy 700s, Regent 1000s, RPM 300s, Modern 20–800s, Recorded in Hollywood 100s, Federal 12100s, RCA 5000s, Crown 100s, Spark 100s, Whippet 200s, Knight 2000s, Arvee 5000s, Vogue 9000s, Atco 6000s, Turntable 500s, Date 1500/1600s, King 6000s, Lon (E) HLE 8000/9000s, HLK 9000s, HLZ 10400s, CBS (E) 2000s, Direction (E) 58–3000s, Par (E) R 5000s, SS (E) 2000s, and Atl (E) 584000s/K 10200s are 78 or 45 rpm singles; Atco EP 4500s, Lon (E) REE 1200s/REK 1300s and Atl (E) AET 6000s are EPs; all other issues are LPs.

Numbers following (E) are British issues.

### THE ROBINS

*The Four Bluebirds*

Bobby Nunn (lead bass), Ty Terrell (tenor), Roy Richards (bari), Billy Richards (bari) with Devonia Williams (p), Pete Lewis (g), Mario De la Garde (b), Johnny Otis (dm).

*Los Angeles 1947*

| | | |
|---|---|---|
| C 540 A | My Baby done told me | Excelsior 540, Californian 301 |
| C 540 B | Court room Blues | Excelsior 540, Californian 301 |

*The Robins*

(vo), Mickey Champion on 1? with p, g, b, dm

| | | |
|---|---|---|
| | | *Los Angeles 1949* |
| | Round about Midnight (BB 5/49) | Score 4010, Imperial LM 94005 |
| | You sure look good to me —1 | Score 4010, Imperial LM 94005 |
| | Don't like the way you're doing (BB 9/49) | Aladdin 3031 |
| | Come Back Baby | Aladdin 3031 |

*The Robins*

Bobby Nunn (lead bass), Ty Terrell (tenor), Roy Richards (bari), Billy Richards (bari) with Devonia Williams (p), Johnny Otis (vbs), Pete Lewis (g), Mario De la Garde (b), Leard 'Kansas City' Bell (dm). Produced by Ralph Bass.

| | | |
|---|---|---|
| | | *Radio Recorders, Los Angeles 1949* |
| SLA 4445 | There's Rain in my Eyes | Savoy 752 |

*The Robins*

(vo), Esther and Bobby Nunn duet on —1 with same acc.

| | | |
|---|---|---|
| | | *Radio Recorders, Los Angeles, Nov. '49* |
| SLA 4452-1 | If it's so Baby (BB 12/49) | Savoy 726 |
| SLA 4453 | Our Romance is gone | Savoy 738 |
| SLA 4454 | If I didn't love you so | Savoy 726 |
| SLA 4455 | | (u) |
| SLA 4456 | Double Crossing Blues —1 | Savoy 731 |
| 2 × 20 | (BB 1/50) | |

*Note:* Savoy 731 was issued with two items on rev. 'Back Alley Blues' by The Beale Street Gang and 'Nothin' Shakin' by Leon Sims.

*The Robins*

Bobby Nunn (lead bass), Ty Terrell (tenor), Roy Richards (bari), Billy Richards (bari), with Don Johnson, Lee Graves (tp), Lorenzo Holden, James Von Streeter (ts), Walter Henry (bs), George Washington (tb), Devonia Williams (p), Pete Lewis (g), Mario De la Garde (b), Leard 'Kansas City' Bell (dm). Orch directed by Johnny Otis.

| | | |
|---|---|---|
| | | *Radio Recorders, Los Angeles, 1950* |
| SLA 5101-3 | The Turkey Hop Pt. 2 | Savoy 732 |
| SLA 5102-3 | The Turkey Hop Pt. 1 | ,, |

*The Robins*

(vo) with Devonia Williams (p), Pete Lewis (g), Mario De la Garde (b), Johnny Otis (vbs), Leard 'Kansas City' Bell (dm). Produced by Ralph Bass

| | | *Radio Recorders, Los Angeles, 1950* |
|---|---|---|
| SLA 5108-2 | I'm Through | Savoy 762 |
| SLA 5109 | I'm living OK (BB 6/50) | Savoy 752 |
| SLA 5110-1 | There ain't no use Beggin' (BB 4/50) | Savoy 738 |
| SLA 5111 | You're Fine but not my Kind (BB 9/50) | Savoy 762 |

*Johnny Otis Orch.**

With Mel Walker, Esther Phillips (and voc. gp ? The Robins)

| | | *Radio Recorders, Los Angeles, 1950* |
|---|---|---|
| SLA 5114 | Mistrustin' Blues | Savoy 735 |
| SLA 5115-3 | Dreamin' Blues | Savoy 748, Regent 1018 |
| SLA 5116 | Cupid's Boogie | Savoy 750 |

*Note:* Rev. of 735 is 'Misery' (Esther Phillips only); Rev. of 748 is 'Helpless' (Mel Walker only); Rev. of 750 is 'Just can't get Free' (Little Esther and The Beltones).

*The Robins*

(vo) with

| | | |
|---|---|---|
| | I Found Out | Savoy (unissued) |
| | Have a Merry Christmas | ,, |

*The Nic-Nacs*

Bobby Nunn (lead bass), Esther Phillips (lead), Ty Terrell (tenor), Roy Richards (bari), Billy Richards (bari) with ts, p, g, b, dm

| | | *Los Angeles, 1950* |
|---|---|---|
| 1440-2 | Found me a Sugar Daddy (BB 12/50) | RPM 313, 316, 342 |
| 1441-3 | Gonna have a Merry Christmas | ,, ,, |
| 1443-3 | You didn't want my love | ,, |

*Bobby Nunn and the Robbins*

Bobby Nunn (lead bass), Ty Terrell (tenor), Roy Richards (bari), Billy Richards (bari) with vbs, p, b, dm.

| | | *Los Angeles, 1951* |
|---|---|---|
| 1517-2 | Rockin' | Modern 20-807 |
| 1518-2 | That's what the Good Book Says | ,, |

*American discographers regularly list 'Mistrustin' Blues' despite the fact that no vocal group is present. The session is included for that reason.

*The Robins*

Bobby Nunn (lead bass), Ty Terrell (tenor), Roy Richards (bari), Billy Richards (bari), Maggie Hathaway (lead on −1) with

| | | |
|---|---|---|
| | | *Los Angeles ? 1952* |
| | Race of Man | Recorded in |
| | Bayou Baby Blues −1 | Hollywood 112 |
| 4050 | Early Morning Blues | Recorded in |
| 4051 | School Girl Blues | Hollywood 150 |

*Little Esther and Bobby Nunn*

Bobby Nunn (lead bass on −1), with Don Johnson (tp), Eli Wolinsky (ts), Fred Ford (bs), George Washington (tb), Devonia Williams (p), Pete Lewis (g), Mario De la Garde (b), Johnny Otis (vbs), Leard Bell (dm). Produced Ralph Bass. Voc. gp. The Robins or The Jayos.

| | | |
|---|---|---|
| | | *Radio Recorders, LA, 25 July 1952* |
| F-269-1 | Saturday Night Daddy −1 | Federal 12100 |
| F-270-1 | Mainliner | Federal 12100, King LP 622 |
| F-271-1 | You took my love too fast −1 | Federal 12122 |

*Note:* Rev. of 12122 is 'Street Lights' by Little Esther only

*The Robins*

Grady Chapman (lead tenor on −1), Bobby Nunn (lead bass on −2), Ty Terrell (tenor), Roy Richards (bari), Billy Richards (bari) with ts, bs, p, g, b, dm. Orch. dir. by Shorty Rogers.

| | |
|---|---|
| | *Los Angeles, 1953* |
| A Fool such as I −1−2 (BB 2/53) | RCA 5175 |
| My Heart's the Biggest Fool −1 | ,, |
| Oh Why −1−2 (BB 4/53) | RCA 5271 |
| All Night Baby −2 | ,, |
| Let's go to the Dance −2 | RCA 5434 |
| How would you know | ,, |
| Ten Days in Jail* −1 (BB 10/53) | RCA 5489 |
| Empty Bottles −2 | ,, |
| Get it off your Mind −2 (BB 12/53) | RCA 5564 |
| Don't stop Now −1 | ,, |

*Produced by Jerry Leiber and Mike Stoller.

*The Robins* (*As Robbins)
(vo) with

| | | |
|---|---|---|
| | | *Los Angeles, ? 1954* |
| 329 | Double Crossin' Baby —1 (BB 2/54) | Crown 106 |
| 330 | I made a Vow —1—2 | ,, |
| 331 | All I do is Rock* —2 (BB 7/54) | Crown 120 |
| 332 | Key to my Heart* —1 | ,, |

*The Robins*

Carl Gardner (lead tenor), Richard Berry (lead —1), Grady Chapman (lead —2), Bobby Nunn (lead —3), Ty Terrell (second tenor), Roy Richards (bari), Billy Richards (bari) with Gil Bernal (ts), Mike Stoller (p), Barney Kessel or Charlie 'Chuck' Norris (g), Ralph Hamilton (b), Jesse Sailes (d). Produced by Jerry Leiber and Mike Stoller. Engineer: Abe 'Bunny' Robyn.

| | | |
|---|---|---|
| | | *Los Angeles, 1954–5* |
| LS 13 | The Hatchet Man —3 | Spark 116 |
| LS 14 | One Kiss | Spark 113, Atco LP 101 |
| LS 15 | Wrap it Up (BB 6/54) | Spark 103, Atco LP 101 |
| LS 16 | Riot in Cell Block Number Nine —1 | Spark 103, Atco LP 101 LP 143, LP 371, EP 4503, Atl (E) K 30031 |
| LS 21 | Just like a Fool | Spark 122, Atco 6059 |
| LS 22 | Loop de Loop Mambo (BB 10/54) | Spark 107, Atco 6059, EP 4503 |
| LS 23 | I must be Dreamin' | Spark 116, Atco 6059 |
| LS 24 | Framed —3 | Spark 107, Atco 6059, LP 143, EP 4503 |
| LS 27 | | |
| LS 28 | | |
| LS 29 | I Love Paris —2 | Spark 113 |
| LS 30 | Smokey Joe's Cafe (BB 10/55) | Spark 122, Atco 6059, Atco LP 101, LP 371, Atl (E) 587096, Atl (E) K 30031 |
| LS 31 | Whadaya Want —2 (BB 2/55) | Spark 110 |
| LS 32 | If Teardrops were kisses | ,, |

*The Robins*

Grady Chapman (lead), Ty Terrell (tenor), Billy Richards (bari), Roy Richards (bass), H. B. Barnum (utility voice) with tps, tb, ts, bs, p, g, b, dm. Produced H. B. Barnum

| | | |
|---|---|---|
| | *Los Angeles, 1956–7* | |
| Cherry Lips (BB 3/56) | Whippet 200, | WLP 703 |
| Out of the Picture | ,, | ,, |
| Hurt Me (BB 23/6/56) | Whippet 201, | ,, |
| Merry go Rock | ,, | ,, |
| Since I first met You (BB 3/11/56) | Whippet 203, | ,, |

| | | |
|---|---|---|
| | That old Black Magic | Whippet 203, WLP 703 |
| | A Fool in Love (BB 30/3/57) | Whippet 206, ,, |
| | All of a sudden my heart sings | ,, ,, |
| | Every Night | Whippet 208 ,, |
| | Where's the Fire | ,, ,, |
| | In my Dreams | Whippet 211 |
| | Keep your mind on Me | ,, |
| | You wanted Fun (BB 20/1/58) | Whippet 212 |
| | Snowball | ,, |
| | How Long | ,, |

*The Robins*

Grady Chapman (lead), Ty Terrell (tenor), Billy Richards (bari), Roy Richards (bass) with

*Los Angeles, 1958*

| | | |
|---|---|---|
| IM-1708 | A Quarter to Twelve (BB 15/9/58) | Knight 2001 |
| IM-1709 | Pretty Little Dolly | ,, |
| IM-1831 | A little bird told me (BB 8/12/58) | Knight 2008 |
| IM-1832 | It's never too late | ,, |

*The Robins*

(vo) with Grady Chapman (lead) with tb, bs, p, g, f-b, dm. Add cga −1

*Los Angeles, 1960*

| | | |
|---|---|---|
| | Just like That (CB 11/6/60) | Arvee 5001, Vogue (E) |
| | Whole lotta Imagination −1 | 9173, VA-H 8059 |

*Note:* The Robins on Gone (1958), Texas Film (1960), Lavender (1961) Musicor, Push, Sweet Taffy, and Ardent are thought to be different groups.

* * *

## THE COASTERS

*The Coasters*

Carl Gardner (lead tenor), Leon Hughes (tenor), Billy Guy (baritone), Bobby Nunn (bass) with orch. inc. Adolph Jacobs (g), ts, p, b, dm, A Leiber–Stoller production.

*Hollywood Recorders, Los Angeles, 11 January 1956*

| | | |
|---|---|---|
| S-1857 | Brazil | Atco 6073, LP 101 |
| S-1858 | Down in Mexico | Atco 6064, LP 101, LP 111, LP 371, Clarion LP 605, Lon (E) HAE 2237, Atl 590 015 |

| | | |
|---|---|---|
| S-1859 | One kiss led to another | Atco 6073, LP 101, Clarion 605 |
| S-1860 | Turtle Dovin' | Atco 6064, LP 101, LP 371, Atl (E) K30031 |

*The Coasters*

Carl Gardner (lead tenor), Billy Guy (lead baritone —1), Young Jessie (baritone), Bobby Nunn (bass), with Plas Johnson (ts), Mike Stoller (p), Adolph Jacobs, Barney Kessell (g), Ralph Hamilton (b), Jessie Sailes, Alvin Stoller (dm), Joe Oliveira (perc). A Leiber–Stoller production.

*Hollywood Recorders, Los Angeles, 12–15 February 1957*

| | | |
|---|---|---|
| 57c-186 | Sweet Georgia Brown —1 | Atco 6104, LP 111, Lon (E) HAE 2237, Atl 590 015 |
| 57c-187 | Young Blood | Atco 6087, EP 4501, LP 101, LP 111, LP 371, Atl LP 8163, Lon (E) HLE 8450, REE 1203, HAE 2237, Atl 590 015, Atl 587 096, Atl K 30031 |
| 57c-188 | Searchin' —1 | Atco 6087, EP 4501, LP 101, LP 111, LP 143, LP 371, Atl LP 8163, Lon (E) HLE 8450, REE 1203, HAE 2237, HAE 2167, Atl 5004, Atl 584087, Atl 590 015, HAB 8189, Atl 587 096, Atl 587 109, Atl K 30031 |
| 57c-189 | Lola (59c-3689) | LP 101 |

*The Coasters*

Same (vo) with orch. dir. by Jesse Stone: Count Hastings (ts), Kenny Burrell (g), Lloyd Trotman (b), Joe Marshall (dm).
A Leiber–Stoller production.

*New York, 13 June 1957*

| | | |
|---|---|---|
| 57c-241 | My Baby comes to Me —1 | Atco 6098, EP 4501 |

*Note:* This session is listed as it appears in Atlantic's files which suggests that the matrix number on the record (57c-251) is incorrect.

*The Coasters*

Same (vo) with Mike Stoller (p), Adolph Jacobs (g), Willie Dixon or

Louis Myers (b), Fred Below (d), Floyd McDaniels ( ).
A Leiber–Stoller production.

| | | *Chess Studios, Chicago, 24 July 1957* |
|---|---|---|
| 57c-252 | Idol with the Golden Head | Atco 6098, EP 4501, LP 371, Clarion LP 605, Atl (E) K 30031 |
| 57c-253 | What is the secret of your success −1 | Atco 6104 |

*The Coasters*

Carl Gardner (lead tenor), Billy Guy (lead baritone −1), Young Jessie (baritone), Tommy Evans or Bobby Nunn (bass) with Jesse Powell (ts), Mike Stoller (p), Adolph Jacobs, Al Caiola (g), Lloyd Trotman (b), Joe Marshall, Alvin Stoller (dm), Harry Breuer ( ). A Leiber–Stoller production.

| | | *Capitol Studios, New York, 4 December 1957* |
|---|---|---|
| | Wait a Minute (57c-3700) (59c-4083) −1 | Atco 6186, LP 135, Lon (E) HLK 9293, HAK 8033, Atl 588 134 |
| 57c-328 | Dance! | Atco 6111, Clarion LP 605, EP 4507 |
| 57c-329 | Gee Golly −1 | Atco 6111, EP 4507 |

*The Coasters*

Carl Gardner (lead tenor), Cornel Gunter (tenor), Billy Guy (baritone, lead on — 1), Will 'Dub' Jones (bass, lead on — 2) with King Curtis (ts), Mike Stoller (p), Adolph Jacobs, Clifton Best, Alan Hanlon (g), Lloyd Trotman (b), Joe Marshall (dm), Francisco Pozo (bgo). A Leiber–Stoller production.

| | | *New York, 17 March 1958* |
|---|---|---|
| 58c-363 | Zing went the strings of my heart −2 | Atco 6116, LP 111, Lon (E) HLE 8665, HAE 2237, Atl 590 015 |
| 58c-364 | Three Cool Cats | Atco 6132, EP 4506, Clarion LP 605, Lon (E) HLE 8819 |
| 58c-365 | Yakety Yak | Atco 6116, EP 4503, LP 111, LP 143, LP 371, Clarion LP 605, Atl LP 8164, Lon (E) HLE 8665, REE 1203, HAE 2237, HAE 2167, HA 8138, |

| | | |
|---|---|---|
| | | Atl 584087, Atl K 10258, Atl 590 015, Atl 587097, Atl K 30031 |
| 58c-366 | Stewball (59c-4124) —1 | Atco 6168, LP 135, Lon (E) HLK 9151, HAK 8033, Atl 588 134 |

*The Coasters*

Same (vo) with King Curtis (ts), Mike Stoller (p), Adolph Jacobs (g), b, dm. A Leiber–Stoller production.

*New York, 8 August 1958*

| | | |
|---|---|---|
| 58c-419 | Sorry but I'm gonna have to pass (59c-3632) —2 | Atco 6126, EP 4506, Lon (E) HLE 8729 |
| 58c-420 | The Shadow Knows —1 | Atco 6126, EP 4506, LP 111, Lon (E) HLE 8729, HAE 2237, Atl 590 015 |

*The Coasters*

Same (vo) with Taft Jordan, Red Solomon (tp), Eddie Bert (tb), King Curtis (ts), Mike Stoller (p), Adolph Jacobs, Don Arnone (g), Milt Hinton (b), Belton Evans (dm). A Leiber–Stoller production.

*New York, 11 December 1958*

| | | |
|---|---|---|
| 58c-460 | Sexy | (Unissued) |
| 58c-461 | Charlie Brown | Atco 6132, EP 4506, LP 111, LP 143, LP 371, Clarion LP 605, Lon (E) HLE 8819, REE 1203, HAE 2237, HA 8129, Atl 590 015, Atl 5004, Atl 587 097, Atl 587 109, Atl K 30031 |
| 58c-462 | I'm a Hog for You | |
| | Charlie Brown | Atl LP 8164 |

*The Coasters*

Same (vo) with King Curtis (ts), Mike Stoller (p), George Barnes, Alan Hanlon, Tony Mottola (g, bjo), Abie Baker (b), Sticks Evans (dm). A Leiber–Stoller production.

*New York, 26 March 1959*

| | | |
|---|---|---|
| 59c-3418 | Along Came Jones | Atco 6141, EP 4507, LP111, LP 371, Clarion LP 605, Lon |

| | | |
|---|---|---|
| | | (E) HLE 8882, HAE 2237, HA 8148, Atl 590 015, Atl K 30031 |
| 59c-3419 | That is Rock and Roll | Atco 6141, EP 4507, LP 111, Clarion LP 605, Lon (E) HLE 8882, HAE 2237, Atl 590 015 |
| | That is Rock and Roll | LP 371, Atl K (E) 30031 |

*The Coasters*
Same (vo) with 2 g, f-b, dm

*New York, 16 July 1959*

| | | |
|---|---|---|
| 59c-3606 | What About Us | Atco 6153, LP 135, Lon (E) HLE 9020, HAK 8033, Atl 588 134 |
| 59c-3607 | Poison Ivy | Atco 6146, LP 111, Atl LP 8164, Lon (E) HLE 8938, Atl K 10258, HAE 2237, Atl 590 015, Atl 5004, Atl 587 097 |
| | Poison Ivy | LP 371, Atl (E) K 30031 |

*The Coasters*
Same (vo) with King Curtis (ts), Mike Stoller (p), Adolph Jacobs, Mickey Baker, George Barnes (g), Wendell Marshall (b), Alfred Dreares (dm), Willie Rodriguez (bgo). A Leiber–Stoller production.

*New York, 17 July 1959*

| | | |
|---|---|---|
| 59c-3610 | I'm a Hog for You | Atco 6146, LP 111, Lon (E) HLE 8938, HAE 2237, Atl 590 015 |

*The Coasters*
Same (vo) with King Curtis (ts), Mike Stoller (p), Adolph Jacobs, Al Caiola (g), Wendell Marshall (b), Panama Francis (dm). A Leiber–Stoller production.

*New York, 23 July 1959*

| | | |
|---|---|---|
| 59c-3713 | Run Red Run −1 | Atco 6153, LP 135, Lon (E) HLE 9020, HAK 8033, Atl 588134 |

*The Coasters*
Same (vo) with King Curtis (ts), Mike Stoller (p), Sonny Forriest, George Barnes (g), Wendell Marshall (b), Panama Francis (dm). A Leiber–Stoller production.

| | | New York, 26 February 1960 |
|---|---|---|
| 60c-4275 | Besame Mucho Pt 1 (60c-4293) | Atco 6163, Lon (E) HLK 9111 |
| 60c-4275 | Besame Mucho Pt 2 (60c-4294) | Atco 6163, Lon (E) HLK 9111 |
| 60c-4276 | The Snake and the Bookworm | Atco 6178, LP 135, Lon (E) HLK 9208, HAK 8033, Atl 588134 |
| 60c-4277 | Wake me, Shake Me | Atco 6168, LP 135, Lon (E) HLK 9151, HAK 8033, Atl 588134 |
| 60c-4278 | Lady Like | Atco 6341 |

*The Coasters*

Carl Gardner (tenor lead —1), Cornel Gunter (tenor lead —2), Billy Guy (baritone lead —3), Will 'Dub' Jones (bass lead —4) with Ellis Larkins (p), Sonny Forriest, Art Ryerson, Alan Hanlon (g), George Duvivier (b), Don Lamond (dm), Phil Kraus (perc). Orch. dir. by Stan Appelbaum. A Leiber–Stoller production.

| | | *New York, 13 June 1960* |
|---|---|---|
| 60c-4625 | Easy Living —2 | Atco LP 123 |
| 60c-4626 | Don't get around much anymore —3 | ,, |
| 60c-4627 | Moonlight in Vermont —1 | ,, |
| 60c-4628 | Moonglow —1 | ,, |
| 60c-4629 | You'd be so nice to come come home to —4 | ,, |
| 60c-4630 | Autumn leaves —2 | ,, |

| | | *New York, 15 June 1960* |
|---|---|---|
| 60c-4631 | Gee Baby Ain't I good to You —3 | Atco LP 123 |
| 60c-4632 | Satin Doll —1 | ,, |
| 60c-4633 | The way you look tonight —4 | ,, |
| 60c-4634 | Willow weep for Me —1 | ,, |
| 60c-4635 | But Beautiful —4 | ,, |
| 60c-4636 | On the sunny side of the Street —2 | ,, |

*The Coasters*

Carl Gardner (lead tenor), Cornel Gunter (tenor), Billy Guy (baritone, lead on —1), Will 'Dub' Jones (bass) with King Curtis (ts), Mike Stoller (p), Sonny Forriest, Phil Spector (g), Wendell Marshall (b), Gary Chester (dm). A Leiber–Stoller production.

| | | |
|---|---|---|
| | | *New York, 29 July 1960* |
| 60c-4752 | Thumbin' a Ride | Atco 6186, Lon (E) HLK 9293 |
| 60c-4753 | Dog Face | (Unissued) |
| 60c-4754 | Shoppin' for Clothes | Atco 6178, LP 371, Atl (E) K 10258, Atl K 30031 |

*The Coasters*

Same (vo) with

| | | |
|---|---|---|
| 60c-4861 | Keep on Rollin' | Atco 6192, LP 135, Lon (E) HLK 9349, HAK 8033, Atl 588 134 |

*The Coasters*

Same (vo) with Plas Johnson (ts), Jewel Grant (bs), Ernie Freeman (p), Sonny Forriest, Rene Hall (g), Eddie Williams (b), Melvin Pollan (dm). A Sill–Hazelwood (*sic*) production.

| | | |
|---|---|---|
| | | *Los Angeles, 7 December 1960* |
| 60c-5234 | Ridin' Hood | Atco 6219 |

*The Coasters*

Same (vo) with King Curtis (ts), Mike Stoller (p), Sonny Forriest, George Barnes, Alan Hanlon (g), Abie Baker (b), Bob Rosengarten, Gary Chester (dm). A Leiber–Stoller production

| | | |
|---|---|---|
| | | *New York, 9 February 1961* |
| 61c-5330A | Girls, Girls, Girls, Pt. 1 —1 | Atco 6204, LP 135, Lon (E) HLK 9413, HAK 8033, Atl 588 134 |
| 61c-5330B | Girls, Girls, Girls, Pt. 2 —1 | Atco 6204, LP 135, Lon (E) HLK 9413 |
| 61c-5331 | Little Egypt —1 | Atco 6192, LP 135, LP 371, Lon (E) 9349, AET 6006, HAK 8033, Atl 588 134, Atl 587 140, Atl K 30031 |

*The Coasters*

Same (vo) with Steve Douglas (ts), Sandy Nelson (dm), James H. Davids ( ), Michael Adams ( ), Llevellyn Klassy ( ). A Sill–Hazelwood (*sic*) production.

| | | |
|---|---|---|
| | | *Los Angeles, 10 April 1961* |
| 61c-5513 | Giving Up | (Unissued) |

| | | |
|---|---|---|
| 61c-5514 | Hungry —1 | Atco 6341 |
| 61c-5515 | Teach me how to Shimmy —1 | Atco 6219 |
| 61c-5516 | I'm a Humdinger | (Unissued) |

*Note:* Label of 'Hungry' is printed 'Hongry' and erroneously shows a Leiber–Stoller production.

*The Coasters*

Carl Gardner (lead tenor), Earl Carroll (second tenor, lead on —1), Billy Guy (baritone, lead on —2), Will 'Dub' Jones (bass, lead on —3) with The Upsetters: Grady Gaines, Clifford Burks (ts), Mike Stoller (p), Milt Hopkins, Joe Richardson (g), Olsie Robinson (b), Emile Russell (dm), Gary Bell ( ). A Leiber–Stoller production.

*New York, 25 September 1961*

| | | |
|---|---|---|
| 61c-5699 | My Babe | Atco LP 135, Lon (E) HAK 8033, Atl 588 134 |
| 61c-5700 | Bad Blood | Atco 6210, LP 135, Lon (E) HLK 9493, HAK 8033, Atl 588 134 |
| 61c-5701 | Just Like Me | Atco 6210, LP 135, Lon (E) HLK 9493, REK 1390, HAK 8033, Atl 588 134 |

*The Coasters*

Same (vo) with orch. dir. by Alan Lorber: Dud Bascomb, Lamar Wright (tp), Harry DiVito (tb), Mike Stoller (p), Thomas Palmer, Billy Butler, Bucky Pizzarella (g), Al Lucas (b), Gary Chester (dm). A Leiber–Stoller production.

*New York, 31 July, 1962*

| | | |
|---|---|---|
| 62c-6376A | The Climb Pt. 1 | Atco 6234, Clarion LP 605 |
| 62c-6376B | The Climb Pt. 2 (62c-6414) (instrumental) | Atco 6234, Clarion LP 605 |
| 62c-6377 | Bull Tick Waltz —2 | Atco 6251 |

*The Coasters*

Same (vo) with orch. arr-dir. by Teacho Wilshire: Buddy Lucas (ts), Artie Butler (p), Billy Butler, Mimi Roman, Everett Barksdale (g), Russ Saunders (b), Panama Francis (dm). A Leiber–Stoller production.

*New York, 11 January 1963*

| | | |
|---|---|---|
| 62c-6707 | The P.T.A. —2 | Atco 6251 |

*The Coasters*

Same (vo) with King Curtis' Band: Lamar Wright, Elmon Wright (tp), George Matthews (tb), Jimmy Powell (as), King Curtis, Alva McCain, Noble Watts (ts), Paul Williams (bs), George Stubbs (p), Cornel Dupree (g), Jimmy Lewis (f-b), Ray Lucas (dm).

| | | |
|---|---|---|
| | | *New York, Apollo Theatre, 16 November 1963* |
| 63c-7400 | Tain't Nothin' to Me —3 | Atco 6287, LP 159, Lon (E) HLK 9863, HAK 8174, Atl 590007, Atl 587141 |
| 63c-7401 | Speedo's Back in Town —1 | Atco 6287, LP 159, Lon (E) HLK 9863, HAK 8174, Atl 590007 |

*The Coasters*

Same (vo) with orch. arr-dir. by Charles Calello: James Cleveland (tb), Leroy Glover (org), Horace Ott (p), Thomas Palmer, Vincent Bell, Al Gorgoni (g), Russ Saunders (f-b), Buddy Saltzman (dm), George Devens (perc), Joe d'Addario, Raymond Desio, William Outerbridge ( ), Barbara Webb, Maretha Stewart, Eileen Gilbert (vo).

| | | |
|---|---|---|
| | | *New York, 17 December 1963* |
| 63c-7477 | Bad Detective —2 | Atco 6300 |
| 63c-7478 | Lovey Dovey | Atco 6300 |
| 63c-7479 | | |
| 63c-7480 | Skylark | (Unissued) |

*The Coasters*

Same (vo) with orch. arr-dir. by Teacho Wilshire: Bill Bivens (ts), Ernie Hayes (p), Eric Gale, Carl Lynch, Troy Seals (g), Jimmy Lewis (f-b), Bernard Purdie (dm). Co-produced by Gregory Carroll.

| | | |
|---|---|---|
| | | *New York, 28 August 1964* |
| 64c-8153 | Wild One —2 | Atco 6321 |
| 64c-8154 | Speedball | (Unissued) |
| 64c-8155 | I must be Dreaming | Atco 6321 |

*The Coasters*

Same (vo) with orch. arr-dir. by Bert Keyes: Joe Newman, Bill Berry (tp), Buddy Lucas (ts, hca), Seldon Powell (ts), Haywood Henry (bs), Bert Keyes (p), Thomas Palmer, Carl Lynch, Everett Barksdale (g), Bill Winston (f-b), Bobby Donaldson (dm).

| | | |
|---|---|---|
| | | *New York, 21 April 1965* |
| 65c-8832 | Money Honey | Atco 6356 |

| | | |
|---|---|---|
| 65c-8833 | Let's go get Stoned | Atco 6356 |

*The Coasters*

Same (vo) with ts, vbs, g, f-b, dm. Female vocal group —4, hca —5. Billy Guy production.

*New York, September 1965*

| | | |
|---|---|---|
| 65c-9290 | Crazy Baby —2, —4 | Atco 6379 |
| 65c-9291 | Bell Bottom Slacks and a Chinese Kimono (she's my little Spodee-o) —5 | Atco 6379 |

*The Coasters*

Same (vo) with King Curtis' Orch: King Curtis (ts), Paul Griffin (p), Cornell Dupree, Hugh McCracken (g), Chuck Rainey (f-b), Ray Lucas (dm). Produced by King Curtis.

*New York, 26 January 1966*

| | | |
|---|---|---|
| 66c-9877 | She's a Yum Yum | Atco 6407, Atl (E) 584033 |
| 66c-9878 | Saturday Night Fish Fry | Atco 6407, Atl (E) 584033 |
| 66c-9879 | Quicksand | (Unissued) |

*The Coasters*

Carl Gardner (lead tenor), Earl Carroll (tenor), Billy Guy (baritone, lead on —1), Will 'Dub' Jones (bass) with orch. arr-dir. by Mike Stoller with tp, tb, ts, org, p, 2g, f-b, dm. A Leiber–Stoller production.

*New York, 1967*

| | | |
|---|---|---|
| 5916 | Soul Pad (CB 22/4/67) | Date 1552, CBS (E) 2749 |
| 5917 | Down Home Girl —1 | Date 1552, CBS (E) 2749 |

*The Coasters*

Same (vo) with orch. arr-dir. by Artie Butler with tp, tb, ts, org, p, 2g, f-b, Bernard Purdie (dm), bjo, bells, flugelhorn on —2. A Leiber–Stoller production.

*New York, 30 October 1967*

| | | |
|---|---|---|
| CO-98087-2 | She Can | Date 1607, Direction (E) 58-3701 |
| CO-98088 | | |
| CO-98089-1 | Everybody's Woman —1 | Date 1607, Date 1617, Direction (E) 58-3701 |
| | Possibly from the same session: | |
| | D W Washburn —2 | Date 1617 |

Love Potion Number Nine
Cool Jerk
Mustang Sally
On Broadway
Good Lovin'
Mohair Sam
The In Crowd
Down at Poppa Joe's

*The Coasters*

Carl Gardner (lead tenor), Earl Carroll (tenor), Billy Guy or Jimmy Norman (baritone), Will 'Dub' Jones (bass) with
Produced by Lloyd Price, Arthur Jenkins, Jimmy Norman. Arranged by Jerry Thomas.

*Turntable Club, Broadway, New York and Jamaica, ? 1969*

| | | |
|---|---|---|
| T-1000-A | Act Right | Turntable TT 504 |
| T-1001-B | The World is Changing | ,, |

The following titles, previously recorded for Date, have been issued on King with fresh matrices and overdubs including Ronald Bright (bass −1), Taco Meza (flute on −2). Orch. arr. by Marty Sheller and dir. by Larry Harlow on −3. Leiber–Stoller productions.

| | | |
|---|---|---|
| K-13953 | Love Potion Number Nine −1, −2 | King 6385, King LP 1146-498, Par (E) R 5931, Lon HLZ 10437 |
| K-13954 | D W Washburn | King 6385, King 6404, King LP 1146–498, Par (E) R 5931, Lon HLZ 10437 |
| K-13959 | Cool Jerk −3 (RW 8/4/72) | King 6389, King LP 1146-498, SS (E) 2201 |
| K-13960 | Talkin' 'bout a Woman (a.k.a. She Can) | King 6389, King LP 1146-498, SS (E) 2201 |
| K-14182 | Soul Pad | King 6404, King LP 1146-498 |
| | Down Home Girl | King LP 1146-498 |
| | Everybody's Woman | ,, |
| | Mustang Sally | ,, |
| | On Broadway | ,, |
| | Mohair Sam | ,, |
| | The In Crowd | ,, |
| | Down at Poppa Joe's | ,, |

## *Notes*

*Chapter One*

(1) Nik Cohn, '*WopBopaLooBopLopBamBoom*', Paladin, 1970, p. 38.
(2) Johnny Otis, '*Listen to the Lambs*', W. W. Norton and Co., Inc., 1968.
(3) Johnny Otis interviewed by Pete Welding, '*Rolling Stone*', no. 97, 9 December 1971.
(4) Johnny Otis, unpublished interview with Rob Finnis.
(5) Pete Welding, op. cit.
(6) Esther Phillips interviewed by Max Jones, *Melody Maker*, date unknown.
(7) Ty Terrell, unpublished interview with Dick Horlick, February 1971.
(8) Jerry Leiber interviewed by Michael March, *Fusion*, no. 39, 21 August 1970.
(9) Horlick, op. cit.
(10) Bobby Nunn, unpublished interview with Dick Horlick, 29 March 1971.
(11) *Fusion*, op. cit.
(12) Mike Stoller, unpublished interview with Charlie Gillett.
(13) *Fusion*, op. cit.
(14) *Fusion*, op. cit.
(15) Willie Mae Thornton interviewed by Ralph Gleason, Arnold Shaw, *The World of Soul*, Paperback Library, 1971, p. 125.
(16) Ralph Bass interviewed by Michael Lydon, *Greenwood*, Spring 1972.
(17) Horlick, op. cit.
(18) Horlick, op. cit.
(19) Horlick, op. cit.

*Chapter Two*

(1) Richard Berry, unpublished interview with Ron Weiser, September 1973.
(2) Weiser, op. cit.
(3) Weiser, op. cit.
(4) Horlick, op. cit.
(5) Jean Charles Marion, *Record Exchanger*, Volume 2, no. 4, 1972.
(6) *Fusion*, op. cit.

*Chapter Three*

(1) Horlick, op. cit.

(2) *Billboard*, 12 July 1969.
(3) Horlick, op. cit.
(4) Dootsie Williams, *Record Exchanger*, Volume 1, no. 3, 1970.

*Chapter Four*

(1) John Dollard, *Caste and Class in a Southern Town*, Yale University Press, 1937.
(2) *Fusion*, op. cit.
(3) Charlie Gillett, 'Atlantic in the Fifties', *Rolling Stone*, no. 101, 3 February 1972.
(4) Paul Oliver, *Screening The Blues*, Cassell and Co., Inc., 1968, p. 20.
(5) Oliver, op. cit., p. 23.
(6) Nat Hentoff, sleeve-note to Leiber and Stoller's big band album (Atlantic 8047).
(7) John Dunton, *Jazz and Blues*, Volume 2, no. 4, July 1972.
(8) Andrew Weiner, *New Society*, 6 July 1972, p. 27.
(9) Jerry Leiber interviewed by Richard Williams, *Melody Maker*, 29 July, 1972.
(10) Jerry Wexler, 'Clyde McPhatter: Personal Recollection', *Rolling Stone*, no. 113, 20 July, 1972.
(11) Jim Delehant, 'The Rise and Fall of the Vocal Groups', *Crawdaddy*, January 1967.

*Chapter Five*

(1) Jerry Wexler in a letter to Charlie Gillett, 1972.
(2) Jerry Leiber interviewed by Charlie Gillett, 'Honky Tonk', Radio London, 29 July, 1972.
(3) Radio London, op. cit.
(4) The author, *The Drifters: The Rise and Fall of the Black Vocal Group*, Studio Vista, 1971.
(5) Sal Mondrone, Tom Luciani, Steve Flam, Ralph Newman, 'The Cadillacs', '*Bim Bam Boom*', Volume 1, no. 5, April–May 1972.
(6) Curtis Mayfield interviewed by Richard Robinson, Arnold Shaw, *The World of Soul*, op. cit. p. 107.
(7) Frank Zappa interviewed by Richard Williams, *Melody Maker*, 24 August, 1973.

*Chapter Six*

(1) Jerry Leiber interviewed by Peter Burns and Norman Jopling, *Cream*, January 1973.
(2) Jerry Leiber interviewed by Richard Williams, op. cit.
(3) Richard Williams, *Out of His Head—The Sound of Phil Spector*, Outerbridge and Lazard Inc., 1972.
(4) Jerry Leiber interviewed by Richard Williams, op. cit.
(5) *Fusion*, op. cit.
(6) Mike Stoller interviewed by Richard Williams, *Melody Maker*, 29 July 1972.
(7) Jerry Leiber interviewed by Richard Williams, op. cit.